Love and blessings
MaryLouise Ott

Three Husbands and a Lover

THREE HUSBANDS
AND A LOVER

MARY LOUISE OTT

MCP - MAITLAND

Mill City Press, Inc.
2301 Lucien Way #415
Maitland, FL 32751
407.339.4217
www.millcitypress.net

© 2017 by Mary Louise Ott

Printed in the United States of America

ISBN-13: 978-1-54560-186-0

TABLE OF CONTENTS

DEDICATION

T he book is about the life of the most incredible and remarkable woman I have ever known, MaryLouise Ott. The ideas,
thoughts, and stories were written by her, and compiled and orga-
nized by Merridawn Duckler (friend of Mary Louise's) and myself.

My relationship with her spans over 60 years. When I was 6
my dad gave piano lessons on Saturdays and I would often go with
him. There was one particularly cute 5-year-old girl with blond hair
and blue eyes named MaryLouise that caught my attention. That
was only the beginning; through the years we attended Mt. Tabor
Church together, sang in the choir, participated in the church high
school youth group, and attended Portland State together. My heart
would always do a flip-flop when I was near her and to this very day
that has never changed.

Through the years, I have had the privilege of seeing the world
through her eyes, and for the past 19 years being part of her daily
life, and it's been magical. Mary Louise's essence is beauty. She has
always succeeded in making the world a more beautiful place- her
lovely smile, her art projects (she is a truly gifted artist), and our
home and garden is a work of art and beauty. For my Birthday's,
Christmas's, and Anniversary's she would make a beautiful piece of
artwork with words that expressed how deeply she loved me.

MaryLouise and I are so close that we have been described as
bookends, and as being one. We made the perfect couple she was
the brains and I did whatever she asked. Mary Louise and I had so
much fun together, and we could almost read each other's thoughts.
Our love for each other can't be described it's far beyond words. We
would be very content to sit side by side not saying a word, just
holding hands. At night, we would snuggle up in bed together and
comment that life doesn't get any better than this. There is a small

pillow in our bedroom that says, "Happiness is being married to your best friend" and it is certainly true for us.

MaryLouise died on December 18ᵗʰ 2015 after a brief and unexpected illness. No one can possibly fathom how much I will miss our walks, our talks, the quiet companionship, and the warmth of her touch, her kisses, her beautiful eyes, which often sparkle, and her smile. Some of her last words to me were, "I love you more than anything in all of creation". That also sums up my feelings for her.

Mary Louise will always be in my heart and part of my soul. Love is stronger than death and someday we will be together again. I will see you soon sweetheart. My dearest this book is in memory of you! With All My Affection and Love, Friends and Lovers Forever Gary

Wisdom is radiant and unfading,
she is easily discerned by those who love her, and is found by those
who seek her.
She hastens to make herself known to those who desire her.

The Book of Wisdom 6: 12–13 NRSV

CAST OF CHARACTERS

There were many friends and relatives Mary Louise loved, however the following people are the principal characters in her life and this is how she described them:

MaryLouise Ott (born 1950 died 2015) – The protagonist

Child: quiet, reserved, happiest playing with dolls & drawing, low self-esteem, good student, creative, few friends, awkward, sensitive, need to please, blond hair, blue eyes, cute

Adult: creative/artistic, a romantic, need for solitude, hard-working, perfectionist, spiritual, dependable, intelligent, independent, assertive, engaged with people and passions, compassionate, love to laugh, sense of humor, 5'-3", reddish hair, fiery, mechanically inclined, problem solver, artist, interior designer, art educator

Melba Bethine Roscoe McAllister Ott (Beth) (born 1920 died 2000) – Mary Louise's mother Positive outlook, loved to laugh, warm smile, hard-working, strong, quick, independent, liked things just so, kind, compassionate, take charge & make things happen, great cook, seamstress, homemaker, playful with children, 5'-2", dark wavy hair, blue eyes, beautiful, open minded

Joseph M. McAllister (Joe) (born 1916 died 1945) – My mother's 1st husband, Judy's father. Unseen member of family, tall, dark hair, handsome features, gentle smile, kind, man's man, serious & fun loving, protective, deeply in love with Beth & Judy, factory worker, pilot in WWII

Judy McAllister Orem (born 1944 –) My half-sister, six years older lives to talk & laugh, political conservative, needs to be in charge, needs attention, lifelong sibling conflict, 5'-2", dark hair, blue eyes, attractive in her youth, housewife, leukemia.

Roland Elwood Ott (born 1917 died 2012) – My mother's second husband, my father, stern, rigid, religious, intelligent (2 master's degrees), mechanical engineer, inventor, balding, glasses, medium height, nerdy, obsessive, Asperger's.

Mae Belle Scott Roscoe born 1897 died 1979 – My maternal grandmother, serious, tired, hardworking, soft round body, bushy eyebrows, white & dark hair, wire rim glasses, homemaker, preacher, great cook, seamstress, story teller, loves to talk, warm voice laced with a chuckle, high moral standards

Fenton Guy Roscoe (born 1894 died 1984) – My maternal grandfather, gregarious, positive outlook, hardworking, short & wiry, farmer's hands, gravelly voice, bald, wire rim glasses, farmer, pastor (Elmer Gantry), real estate salesman, entrepreneur

Gary Stanley Howarth (born 1949 –) My best friend and the love of my life, 1st lover (1976 & 1977), 2nd lover (1996), and 3rd husband–married September 7, 1996, 6' – 7", thick dark hair (now salt & pepper), deep brown eyes, bushy eyebrows and moustache, long gentle fingers, goofy, kind, compassionate, infectious smile, fun, loves to laugh, strong, spiritual, intelligent, easy going, independent, police officer, financial consultant.

Michael Jay Small born 1947 – My 1st husband married August 28th 1971 divorced January 1978 6'-2", dark hair, brown eyes, arms too long, feet too big, self-centered, irresponsible, political liberal, minister, crazy about sports, disorganized, risk taker.

Richard Lynn Katz born 1948 – My 2nd husband married March 28, 1981 divorced August 1996, 5'-7", thick dark curly hair, sharp features, serious, awkward, nerdy, needs routine, slow, intelligent, obsessive interests in wine, history, and classical music, responsible, wine steward, secular Jew.

Aaron Ott Katz born 1981 – My son with Richard.

CAST OF CHARACTERS

Rebecca Ott Katz born 1989 – My daughter with Richard.

Shannon Burrough born 1950 – Gary's 2nd wife.

Gary Stanley Howarth II born 1984 – Gary's son with Shannon.

Alice Boczkaj born 1949 – My college roommate and lifelong friend.

Fun, eccentric, big personality, compassionate, people person, true friend, creative

My aunt and uncles (Beth's sisters and brothers) – Wendel, Paul, Mary, Dorothy, John, Janet, Blythe Dolores Utz – a very special friend who was like a daughter in the latter part of my life.

Other significant friends – Bernice (junior high & high school), Darey (college), Jonny (1st divorce), Mary Elizabeth (1977+), Ruth (1993+)

MEMOIR
INTRODUCTION

D on't call me Mary. The name is Mary Louise. A child of nineteen-fifty middle class America, I fill the role of daughter, granddaughter, sister, friend, wife, ex-wife, mother, stepmother, artist, storyteller, threshold between past and future. Open the door—stroll through me to explore a story from the past written for the future.

My naïve view of the world and low self-esteem grew out of a protected childhood, an observer personality, an overbearing older sister, a narrow-minded father, and school experience dominated by bullying. I was always happier in my own fantasy than the noisy, rough and tumble world of my peers. Playing quietly with my dolls or creating something beautiful with my hands held my attention for uninterrupted hours of bliss. When I did engage with people, I preferred adults to children.

I was an obedient child in an ultra-conservative home dominated by a fundamentalist father. Behind the scenes of that life, my mother's independent spirit created a safe place for me to be myself. She nudged me into the world and acted as a safety net when experiences overwhelmed. She served as a model of common sense, self-sufficiency, and compassion. I would not be who I am without the gentle mentoring of my mother.

Because my mother was a central figure in my life, her story was a powerful force. Mother's childhood was spent taking care of three brothers and three sisters. Her charismatic father, farmer turned preacher, ascribed to the power of positive thinking. Her overworked mother filled in gaps no thought, regardless of power, could plug. The household fueled by toil instead of cash depended on my mother's good heart and efficiency.

At the age of nineteen, Mother was rescued from the drudgery of never finished labor by Joe, the love of her life. When they married, she moved from a position of family servant to cherished partner. Her dream come true ended after six years of marriage when Joe was killed in a B17 bomber crash one month before the end of WWII. Two years after Joe's death, motivated by concern about how to care for herself and her three-year-old daughter, my mother married my father not for love, but for security. I was born three years later.

My tale is a journey from a traditional 1950s childhood, through years of upheaval and three marriages to reach a place of wholeness. I found my way in large part because of the influence of two resilient women, my mother and my maternal grandmother. Our stories are intertwined.

MY MOTHER

M elba Bethine (Beth) Roscoe McAllister Ott, was born on a Montana homestead in 1920. Beth was the eldest girl of seven children. Her family soon moved to Illinois where her father (Fenton) pursued training for the ministry. Three years later Beth's family moved back to Montana where they led a nomadic life even spending a summer in a tent, until her father was called to a church in Beach, North Dakota.

In 1933 the family moved to SE Portland where Beth's father was assigned to a missionary church. With so many children and so much responsibility my mother missed a day of school each week to help her mother (Mae) with household chores. Beth met the love of her life, Joe McAllister, at her father's church. She was 19 when they were married. After America entered WWII, Joe volunteered for the Army Air Force and Beth followed him from base to base during his training. My sister Judy was born during those years. In 1944/45 after Joe was sent to England to fly B17 bombers over Germany, they exchanged almost daily letters about their separate lives and their desire to be together again. Joe died in a plane crash one month before the end of the war. After the war, Beth built a house for herself and her daughter four blocks away from her family home. My father, Roland Ott, joined her there in 1947. They met at my grandfather's church. I was born three years later.

My mother was known for her work ethic, warm hospitality, and open mind as well as her excellent cooking, sewing, and gardening skills. Mother, a saintly force of nature, was 80 when she died of Lymphoma.

MY GRANDMOTHER

Mae Belle Scott Roscoe, was born in a Montana coal-mining town in 1897. The eldest of eight children Mae grew up in Kendall, Montana, a boom town established in the early 1900s when gold was discovered. Mae's blacksmith father was an Irish immigrant from Belfast. Her mother, born in Belfast, Maine, came west with her family in the 1870s.

My grandmother collected post cards sent to her by friends and family from 1907 to 1914 (the golden age of the postcard). The messages on these cards give a glimpse of her happy childhood. At eighteen, Mae taught eight grades of homestead children in a one room log cabin school. During this time, she met her husband, Fenton Guy Roscoe, at a country dance. She was 20 when they were married in 1917 and took up residence on a central Montana homestead.

Grandma Roscoe was known for her work ethic and unbending Christian values as well as her excellent cooking, sewing, and storytelling skills. In the 40s and 50s she worked at Meier & Frank to help support the family. Born before the automobile, she never learned to drive. Grandma, a prickly force of nature, was 82 when she died of Leukemia.

MY NEIGHBORHOOD AND HOME

My family has lived in the same SE Portland neighborhood since 1933, berry fields and orchards dominated the landscape. Until 1950, my grandfather pastured his cow on the land where my home sits. For the first 10 years of my life my grandparents lived four blocks away. Grandpa Roscoe's United Brethren Church was a four-block walk in the opposite direction. Kellogg Grade School, not far from the church, and Franklin High School, an easy walk West on Woodward Street, graduated Roscoe family members from the 1930s until I finished eighth grade in 1964 and my last year of high school in 1968.

Our home is south of Mt. Tabor. Gary grew up one mile from here on the north side of Mt. Tabor. In 1954 we both attended the preschool that was located in the home next door to my house. When I was five and he was six, he sat in the big chair in our living room on Saturday mornings during my piano lesson with his father. We were good friends in high school and college.

I lost my virginity in this house one month before I married Michael, my first husband. While we fumbled with each other in the basement, my mother called down from the top of the stairs to say it was time for Michael to go home. Did she know? I married Richard, my second husband in the living room of this house. In celebration of our marriage, wine was served for the first time inside these walls.

My childhood home is the place that nurtured me. It is also a symbol of personal transformation and integration of my past and present life. Near the end of my fifth decade Gary, my third husband, and I returned to the three-bedroom cape cod style house designed by my father in 1950. The house was built the year I was born it might be said we were both under construction at the same time.

The sound of my feet on the stairs or the twang of a closet door latch; the smell of the inside of my grandmother's china cupboard; the shape of lamps or clocks inherited from my mother and grand-mother; the taste of raspberries from the garden; the feel of the metal stair railing – living in this house again fills my senses and my body resonates with memory.

I have come around full circle. I have come home. The story is about how I got here.

THE OBJECT OF STORIES

My home is a museum of sorts. Not like Alice's cabinet of curiosities where every corner is overflowing with a mixture of elegant or bizarre items she has been collecting since before we were roommates in college. No stuffed Iguanas in my living room. Mine is more of a personal and family history archive, a storehouse of precious objects holding stories as far back as great grandparents and forward through me to the children. Even my 1950s Cape Cod style house has a story – I was three months old the first time I moved in.

Nothing goes in or out of here by accident. I gave Mother's delightful amber Depression glass citrus juicer to Elizabeth for her birthday because I knew she would cherish it as she does my son Aaron. Sometimes things leave as a way to let go of a memory. It was time for the beautifully carved cuckoo clock to go away when I no longer wanted a constant reminder of husband #1. Speaking of husbands, I've lost custody of several treasures although shrewd exchanges were made to keep fine pieces such as the Oriental design rug and the Art Nouveau wardrobe. A too-heavy-to-lift statue of Pan, now sitting by the fireplace, was retrieved from Gary's wife #2 after years of negotiation. According to family legend, his eccentric mother, Nina, liberated the mythical flute player from a garden on King Hill in the 1940s.

I must admit to a weakness for chairs – nearly twenty different styles can be found in various rooms. The big chair in the living room is here for sentimental reasons while others have been added simply because they are classics. I recall the time ten years ago, when I suddenly stopped the car at the corner of Winslow Way and Madison after noticing two rattan chairs on the sidewalk in front of Pastiche. It was easy to see they were real Palecek Bistro chairs not the cheap Ikea knockoffs. Two for half the cost of one – a perk from our time living on an island populated by people with big pocket books and a short attention span. To sit in the chair with the back curving gently down to a comfortable armrest is suggestive of spooning with a lover.

One notion I can't grasp is how someone could abuse and then abandon a battered sofa at the curbside with a sign shouting FREE. My classic tuxedo style sofa will be thirty next year and it still looks as young as the day it arrived. Also, difficult to comprehend is the fact that Janet, my youngest aunt, amputated the legs from my maternal grandmother's buffet so she could use it as a trunk in a spare room. I cry inside when I think of the once proud piece in Mae Belle's dining room where in better days, the center drawer often held a Whitman Sampler. I remember the chatter from the kitchen where Mae Belle and her four daughters were discussing the pros and cons of browning the flour for gravy; cousin Mike stacking olives snitched from the divided dish on each of his fingers; Wendell and Terry jockeying to carve the turkey; all while I sneaked the buffet drawer open just far enough to lift the Sampler lid revealing a handy diagram of flavors, always hoping for one more dark chocolate filled cream.

When I open the doors of Mae Belle's walnut china cupboard and take in the spiciness—it comforts me like the familiar scent of a mother's perfume. As a child, I was enthralled with the contents especially a dainty teacup—Grandma would tip it to the light revealing the face of a geisha at the bottom. She vowed the 1920s china cupboard, table and six chairs I fancied would be mine someday, but if Grandpa's new wife had her way, the set would have been sent to join the sad buffet. Only my bold and bossy older sister Judy could arrive at Fenton's house with a trailer in tow to rescue Mae Belle's dining set for me without anyone mounting a challenge. Judy has the teacup.

On tables at each end of the sofa in my living room sit two lamps as different as the original owners yet each offering similar illumination. The smaller of the two is an antique brass triple branched candelabrum topped with a domed metal shade. Rising above the burgundy colored dome is a brass rod with a ball finial and arrow resembling a weather vane. Mae Belle treasured this fine somewhat impractical lamp because it was a present from her eldest son,

Wendell. Grandma, like the metal lamp, was solid and unbending – she knew where she had been and where she was going as though an arrow pointed the way. The little metal arms precariously supporting the shade are still wrapped in Band-Aids placed there by Grandma to keep the shade from slipping. Each time I right it after a stranger tips it sideways, I think of how pleased she would be to see her remedy still in place.

The other lamp, a tall exquisite white porcelain urn painted with cascading branches covered in delicate deep pink dogwood blossoms and gold leaves, is no longer topped with the overly large and gaudy shade it came with when Mother, bursting with excitement, brought the less than practical prize home from a sale. Beth was as beautiful as her lamp, extraordinary in character, playful in spirit, and would never shy away from making an audacious statement. At the last minute during the estate sale, I saved the lamp and replaced the original shade with one in burgundy and gold silk complimenting the Asian simplicity of the lovely urn. Beth wouldn't mind about the new shade; she wasn't bound by the past.

I proudly display an anniversary clock on the piano that doesn't keep time. It was a gift from Mother inspired by my childhood fascination with the around-and-back movement of shiny brass balls under the glass dome of a similar clock belonging to old family friends. Across the room, Beth's mantel clock sits in the same spot above the fireplace where it has remained for more than sixty years even though the hands have been stopped at ten o'clock for who knows how long. I can still hear the bong, bong, bong of the Westminster chime that drove Beth nuts. There are clocks for telling time and clocks for telling stories.

FAIRY TALE

Joe's photo hung on the wall in the room where I played as a child and his memory permeated our family life. A symbiotic relationship with my mother meant her pain was my pain. When she grieved for Joe, I grieved for Joe. I consciously decided to relive my mother's love story with hope of a different outcome.

Due to growing up in the 1950s and 1960s, my only exposure to love was through the Jane Austin and Louisa May Alcott genre of novels. I knew nothing about dating or sex. I expected to be introduced to the prince charming God intended for me then after a platonic courtship, marry and live happily ever after, end of story.

In the spring of 1965 Michael Small walked into my life. I was 14.

I was a freshman in high school when I met Michael at a church youth group retreat. His tall, dark, and clean cut handsome reminded me of Joe in the photo and he appeared to be nothing like my tyrannical father. The three-year age gap and life changing death of his father gave him an appealing outward maturity. He was fun, smart, and the fact that he planned to attend seminary sealed the deal. In the fantasy marriage to Michael I created in my mind, I could be a preacher's wife like my grandmother. It took three years of flirting and a Gloria LaVonne makeover before he noticed me.

When we began dating in my senior year of high school, I felt Michael was a prize for which I should be forever grateful. A college man lowered himself to notice insignificant me. I can see now how this allowed him to control me. At the time, I thought I was in love. No evidence otherwise, no warning from family or friends, no inner wondering would steer me away from my destiny.

The crazy part of this is that I didn't see how much I had going for me. I was top of my class, creative, attractive, and fun to be with in situations where I felt comfortable. The Gloria LaVonne training and experiences in Europe gave me confidence and fostered independence. Recruited by prestigious Eastern schools I settled for Portland State because I couldn't stand the thought of being so far away from Michael. Looking back, I can see countless possibilities I could have explored if I had not been so obsessed with him.

Part of the allure of my relationship with Michael was bucking my father's rigidity. I was able to get out from behind Dad's view of the world and was introduced to an abundance of pleasure for the first time. Unlike my contemporaries, I didn't join the hippy movement to rebel; I joined the Michael movement. He exposed me to sex, music, food and wine, places, political perspectives and experiences that were new, exciting, and not too far outside my comfort zone.

At first Michael was attentive. We went to movies, events at Lewis & Clark, he took me to the senior prom, and we spent time at his house or my house. Gradually over time he started to expect me to be available when he wanted and disappear when he didn't. He and his family criticized and ridiculed my family's conservative views. His self-centered needs and those of his family took precedence over my needs. I was so "in love" and eager to please that I made myself over into the person I thought was expected. I was color blind to red flags.

I was physically attracted to Michael and his physical attraction to me made me feel special. As our relationship moved from kissing and holding hands to petting, my body was aroused in ways I never imagined. The danger of exploring each other held power. The limitation of not going all the way held power. Sex with Michael before we had intercourse was more satisfying than anything after. For him sexual pleasure started on the honeymoon, for me it ended on the honeymoon. He made it clear that if I was not turned on by sixty second sex with no foreplay it was my problem not his.

As time went on Michael's liberal ideas became more liberal. His original plan to attend seminary in San Francisco was replaced by a desire to study at McCormick Theological Seminary in Chicago because it was more liberal. The minister at our church tried to deny Michael the opportunity to preach given to seminary students who were members because of Michael's liberalism. One summer Sunday morning I accosted Dr. Russell between services and insisted that he allow Michael to preach. He did two weeks later.

I cherished every gift Michael gave me even if it was cheap or ugly. I wore a tacky costume jewelry heart even after all the finish wore off. I made a skirt to wear with an unflattering bright pink sweater he gave me that was scratchy against my skin. My engagement ring, made from his mother's stones, was not the artful design I hoped for, but I never told anyone about my disappointment. Michael and his family thought sentimentality was a weakness. One Mother's Day when his mom received a bouquet of roses from her future son-in-law she chastised him for wasting money on something so frivolous and unnecessary.

I hand knit sweaters for Michael in elaborate patterns, wrote poems and special song lyrics for him such as *Bridge Over Troubled Waters* in calligraphy, handmade cards, and surprised him with treats. I designed a one of a kind wedding ring for him.

I gave myself over to a love fantasy, a mantle of romance placed on Michael that hid his true character. The fantasy distracted me from recognizing the incompatibility of our personalities. We were both young, naïve, and had no experience with or understanding about a committed loving relationship.

In 2008 Gary (a sixty-two-year-old remarkable human being), Enrique (a fifteen-year-old leopard gecko Gary's son dropped off for a temporary stay six years ago) and I return to my childhood home. Our three grown children are visitors rather than residents. Rebecca and Aaron, youngest and oldest, are mine. To limit confusion, we refer to Gary's son, two years younger than Aaron, as Gary 2 or Gary the younger. Sixteen years of stirring the pot smoothed out an excess of lumps in our blended family. Gary and I moved into the house fifty-eight years to the day after the first time I arrived in December 1950.

Gary's memories of childhood connect with mine. My family home stands to the south of Mt. Tabor, his family's property bordered on the north side of the park. We attended the same preschool in 1954. A year later Gary, book in hand, and his father, an accomplished pianist, arrived at our front door every Saturday morning for my piano lesson. Friendship and a brother/ sister bond blossomed in a high school youth-group. Gary often arrived at my home around dinnertime enticed by Mother's pies. In typical older brother fashion, Gary enjoyed teasing. He taught me to drive a stick shift on a Mt. Tabor hill and ratted on me when I agreed to dates for the same movie with two different boyfriends two nights in a row. Springtime afternoons at Portland State College, Gary persuaded me to leave pre-architecture studio classes with promises of adventure. We drove around the West Hills in his enormous 1961 white Cadillac searching for interesting old houses. One time, noses to the glass of a Spanish style mansion, the residents peered back at us.

Gary ushered at my first wedding. I poured coffee at his. Six years later, trapped in failed relationships, we engaged in a brief affair. Then he dumped me. We didn't speak for eighteen years. A chance encounter at Fred Meyer in 1995 on Gary's forty-sixth birthday brought us together again. We married less than a year later. Gary says he married me for my inherited pie baker genes. I married him for his sense of humor and his muscle.

We are completing another day of house projects as Jute backed white wool carpet rips into narrow strips when pulled off a crumbled pad in the cozy slopped ceiling room with a tree house feel referred to since childhood as the little room. After weeks of sorting, cleaning, and refurbishing every room in the house, this prime space above the kitchen, last used as my father's office, is one of the final major projects. My husband drags carpet and pad into a pile then he pauses to look around, "I sense your mother in this room. "Yes, I feel her too." I take in the little room and the unobstructed view of Douglas fir covered Mt. Tabor Park above crowded rooftops. The room and the view tug at my heart. My husband carries carpet and pad fragments out to the garage while I pry up staples, carpet tack strips, and nails. The tedium allows my mind to wander. Memory fragments pile up on top of carpet debris.

After an arduous day of work Gary drapes his six foot seven fleece covered frame over the full length of a chair and ottoman in our living room. Sixteen inches shorter than Gary, I stretch out on the sofa in sweat pants and tattered shirt with room to spare. Gary taps the arms of his chair, "Can you believe I sat in this chair on Saturday mornings when I was a kid?"

I turn my head and smile at his excitement and his disheveled appearance topped off by more salt than pepper hair in wiry disarray, a trimmed moustache his only tidy feature. Gary's vibrant brown eyes flash enthusiasm in my direction.

"You read books in that chair while I sat next to your Dad on the piano bench right over there." His eyes follow my finger to the piano at the end of the living room. "It isn't the same piano. I learned to play on a baby grand." In place of the grand, long gone to piano heaven due to a cracked soundboard, stands a console piano given to me by Mother more than thirty years ago. "I wonder what time it is."

Gary states the obvious, "None of the clocks in this room work. My stomach feels like dinnertime? Food on his mind, he continues, "I can almost hear your mother prepare pot roast and mashed potatoes in the kitchen while your grandmother sits at the dining room table telling stories about the Montana gold mining town of her childhood and the years she taught in a one room log cabin school."

"I wish I paid more attention to Grandma Roscoe's stories. Do you remember how she folded and refolded her napkin until it was shredded as though searching for a story written on the flimsy paper?" We laugh at the image.

Gary extracts himself from the chair and moves in the direction of the kitchen, "Relax, I'll make dinner. Is spaghetti still okay?

"Anything is okay if you fix it. Do you want me to set the table?"

"Sure, we need wine glasses."

I hear the clatter of Gary working his magic on spaghetti sauce. The sound of dinner preparation like the familiar twang of a metal closet latch or the drum of my feet on the basement stairs resonates in my body. The aroma of rich sauce fills my senses. My nose remembers Sunday dinner as I move toward our dining room to retrieve wine glasses from Grandma Roscoe's walnut china cupboard.

Caught between reality and memory, I set the table while thinking about memories from my childhood.

CHILDHOOD AND ADOLESCENCE MEMORIES

KINDERCOLLEGE

I live in a world of daydreams. It is more interesting and safer than the real world. I play dress up and entertain my dolls for tea in the "little room" upstairs. I hear my mother tell someone on the phone, "She can entertain herself for hours."

There aren't any girls to play with in our neighborhood. Only boys, mean boys. They like to torture me. I am the perfect victim, shy and sensitive.

Next door to our house Mrs. Jarvis runs a musical preschool called Kindercollege. Every morning when the parents drive by with their children I hang over the back of the sofa to watch. Some kids laugh, some scream for mama. Every noon I watch the whole drama in reverse, some laugh and some scream for school. I can't wait until I can join the other children at school.

The first morning of Kindercollege my mother packs green grapes for snack in a little plastic box. She takes my hand and we walk next door. I put my snack on the shelves above the crayon drawers and hang my coat in the cloak room. I can smell the crayons in large square drawers each painted a different color matching the crayons inside. There are eight drawers in all, red, blue, yellow, orange, green, purple, black, and brown. The crayons are fat with round tips.

The teacher sits behind a huge black piano. She makes music by magic. We sit quietly in rows at the long wooden tables with green tops. We sign songs.

When we go out for walks around the neighborhood, we pretend to be a train. Each child holds a knot on a long rope. Our teacher pretends to be the engineer driving the train.

COLORED PENCILS

The green cardboard pencil box stands on the table in front of me. Twelve Eberhard Faber colored pencils call me to apply pencil to paper. The feel of the lead on paper ripples through my fingers, to my arm, to the center of my body. I draw because the feel of pencil on paper satisfies me.

Not every pencil is the same. Some are so hard that only a hint of color stays on the paper. It is the soft ones that speak to me. The ones that break when I press down hard. The soft pencils smear intense color across the page.

I've always wanted to be an artist. I draw pictures on little pieces of paper when I'm waiting for grownups to do all the things grownups do. My favorite subject is a lake with mountains in the background, trees on each side, and a sailboat floating in the middle.

Mother and Daddy took me to see a Vincent van Gogh exhibit at the Portland Art Museum. Some of the drawings scared me because they were dark and the people, called potato eaters, looked sad, but other paintings were filled with beautiful colors. I like how the paint is thick and bumpy. The sunflowers are my favorite. When I go home I will draw flowers instead of lakes.

MY SCAR

An aerial view of Crater Lake has been tattooed on my left knee since the summer I turned sixteen and finally passed typing after my third try. Blissfully riding home from Bernice's house one day dreamy afternoon, I turned onto a newly oiled and graveled street where I was instantly snatched back to reality by the familiar sensation of bicycle tires skidding out of control. Two days later, flat on my back, I was held captive while Doctor Rippey, a scalpel in hand, sliced, scraped, and sterilized each gravel and dirt filled laceration on my knee, elbow, and palms. Mother was standing at my feet with her hands gently resting on my ankles; I could only imagine the worried look on her face each time I flinched. In introverted resolve I was mute, concentrating on the coolness of Mother's hands instead of the burning pain of surgical metal against tender flesh. The only sound in the room for what seemed like hours was the clatter of gravel bits dropping into a metal tray. When at long last I was released from confinement on the exam table, everyone seemed amazed to see my back and the sheet soaked with sweat. No one questioned why the doctor neglected to suggest an anesthetic.

I can draw the complex veins of a leaf or the unique texture of a stone with photographic precision, but large motor skills have never been my strength. Always the last one chosen for the softball team, the awkward swimmer who was afraid of the deep end of the pool, the "A" student with a "C" in PE. In sixth grade, I flunked the new physical fitness test imposed on us because President Kennedy thought Americans were soft and out of shape. Rea Wheeler could pop up and down like a spring doing 36 sit-ups in the time I struggled with five. Mother probably tried to reassure me with something like, "no one is good at everything, but everyone is good at something." I appreciated her effort even though I wasn't convinced by her claim.

While the visible scars of childhood often fade, a sound, a smell, a place can unexpectedly prick a memory reopening real or imagined wounds. One evening, walking

through a church parking lot in the neighborhood where I grew up, an almost forgotten fire escape returned me to a day when bicycle tires were fat and no one thought about wearing a helmet.

I cautiously parked my bike next to others scattered in the parking lot and watched the kids swarming around a metal fire escape thinking it wouldn't hurt to join in the game for just a few minutes even though none of the children were my usual playmates. It wasn't the kids that were drawing me in; they seemed much too wild to appeal to a timid eight-year-old. It was the magic of the spacious metal platform standing on spider legs at the top of an inviting stair. In my imagination, such a place could be the deck of a ship, a stage, or a playhouse perched in a tree.

I don't know what tempted me to ride around to the back of the new Baptist Church – we were Presbyterian. The most direct four-block route to Grandma's house, where I had been sent by Mother to borrow some essential ingredient for dinner, would have been to continue on sixty-seventh in front of the building. From that side, the fire escape and the noisy children would have been blocked from view. Maybe I was lured in by the smooth surface of the freshly poured asphalt parking lot where I could ride my bike without worry.

Whatever the reason for my detour, the game of pirates or performers I joined on the enchanted fire escape, made me forget the time and my errand. Suddenly a vision of my Mother patiently waiting for me to return flashed across my mind. With a sick feeling in my stomach I jumped on my bike, pedaling frantically the last half block past the cherry orchard to Grandma's driveway. Much to my horror, the combination of panic, speed, and loose gravel kept me from safely negotiating the last turn. I was helpless as the tires of my bike skidded sideways throwing me face first onto the sharp rock studded ground. Stunned by the impact for a brief moment I was frozen. Somehow, in a blur of blood and tears, I picked myself up and found my way into the comfort and inevitable reproach of Grandma's kitchen.

What a sight I was the next morning at church with partially formed scabs from chin to forehead. I held the bulletin in front of my face to cover my shame. I wonder if that was the time Mother told me the story about her gold-rimmed front tooth. "When I was your age, Wendell thought he would teach me to ride by putting me on a bike at the top of a hill and giving me a shove. I broke my tooth and my glasses. I was a mess." It was hard to believe my invincible mother was ever a mess.

The unfortunate incident in Grandma's driveway wasn't my first bicycle accident and the oiled street disaster wasn't my last. I read somewhere recently that twenty percent of all bicycle crashes involve railroad tracks, wet leaves, or loose gravel. I've done all three – more than once.

EGGS AND RELIGION

The irresistible aroma of Saturday morning breakfast reaches my hungry nose long before I arrive in the kitchen. Is Mother mixing up waffles or pancakes to go along with the bacon calling me to the table?

"Good morning sweetie. Can I tempt you with an egg this morning?"

"Eggs, I don't eat eggs. I was hoping for waffles."

"I keep asking in case there is a miracle and you decide to try a taste."

Even though the answer every Saturday for all of my eight years has been no eggs, on this Saturday morning something about the smell of the crispy edged eggs sizzling in the pan tempts me to say, "I'll try a bite."

Mother in a red and white cherry printed apron over a home-made housedress does an exaggerated flip of the spatula, "This is a historic day." Then gives me a kiss on the forehead before she announces, "Breakfast is ready!"

"I jostle past my older sister to take my seat at the kitchen table in the corner across from Daddy. Because of the refrigerator at my back, the wall on one side and Judy on the other, I'm a prisoner in my seat.

As usual, Daddy prays a long time over our breakfast.

Mother nudges him, "Hurry up Roland the food is getting cold."

I peak through eye slits at Mother and Daddy across the table and an egg in the middle of my plate wondering if the blessing will improve the flavor.

The praying finished, I take a tentative bite. It's a disappointment. The texture is rubbery and it doesn't taste yummy like it looked in the pan. For a moment everyone is too occupied with bacon, eggs, grapefruit, and homemade cinnamon rolls to notice me push my egg around the plate trying to look like I'm eating.

Then comes the dreaded question, "How do you like the egg sweetie?"

I can't lie to my mother, "It doesn't taste as good as it looks. I tried a bite, is that enough?

Before Mother answers, Daddy declares, "Your mother cooked the egg because you asked for it – you will eat the whole thing."

There is nothing that brings out my inherited stubbornness more than an order from Daddy. "I will NOT eat the egg. It's yucky."

In what seems like one continuous movement, Daddy, red faced, erupts from his chair, rushes around the table, reaches over Judy, grabs me by the arm, pulls me out of my chair, and drags me down the hall to my parent's bedroom smacking my bottom with the full force of his hand.

Mother runs down the hall after us shouting, "Roland stop hitting her. She doesn't have to eat the egg." She manages to pull him off of me leaving finger shaped hot welts on my arms and bottom and uncontrollable sobs in my throat.

This isn't the first time Daddy lost his temper. Mother says he has a short fuse. I try to stay out of the way and be invisible, but Judy does the opposite. A few months ago, she made up a song when she discovered the dinner menu included corn for the third or fourth time in a week. "Corn, corn, corn, all we eat is corn." Daddy threw her over his knee and spanked her while she laughed like a crazy person. Mother stopped him. I don't know how Judy manages to laugh. It makes Daddy angrier. Maybe she does it to get back at him because she is spanked so often. He says he is hard on Judy because he feels obligated to Joe, her Daddy, to raise her right.

It may not have been the first time, but it was one of the last I remember. Following the egg episode, it seemed like Daddy was gone more–teaching and taking classes at Portland State in the evenings after work.

For most of my childhood and young adult years, I thought Daddy was an awkward, misunderstood genius. When he was twenty he invented a door latch on the same September 1937 day FDR's motorcade drove from the dedication of Timberline Lodge down Powell Boulevard, a short walk from my Daddy's childhood home. Many years later he bought our 1955 Mercury Mont Claire with the proceeds from selling his latch patent.

Everyone considered Daddy odd and avoided him because he was preachy about religion and would go on for hours talking about his wild ideas and inventions. Even though his explanations were hard to follow, I pretended to understand his theories about electricity and gravity. My reward was praise for a special intellect, which made me feel as though he loved me.

It wasn't until a few years before his death that I stumbled onto the source of my father's narcissism, lack of empathy, and obsessive behavior. I now believe he suffered from an undiagnosed developmental disorder related to Autism called Asperger's Syndrome. This discovery at an earlier time could have transformed his life and mine.

RECIPE FOR SUCCESS

Every school day at 11:30 I walk four blocks down SE Franklin Street to 65th then turn right and walk three more blocks to my house where Mother and I eat lunch together. I think about lunch all morning and feel sad when it is over. Not just because the food is delicious. Lunch is my safe place away from school and my time to be with Mother all by myself.

Today is Tuesday, leftover biscuits and gravy, my favorite. If I'm lucky, Mother baked cookies this morning. The warm scent of comforting food greats my nose and the familiar sound of the radio fills my ears when I open the back door. I can use some comfort today. Two boys teased me on the way home and my new teacher is scary.

Mother is standing at the stove warming lunch. Fresh cookies are piled up on the bread board, "How was your morning sweetie?"

"Mike and John followed me down Franklin Street. They called me Ott Snott because I got 100% on my arithmetic."

"I'm sorry they were so mean. You know what they say about sticks and stones. The boys are just jealous. Go wash your hands honey. Lunch is ready."

Mother says words don't hurt, but they do. I wish I could let them "roll off my back" the way she does.

Back at the table with clean hands I dig into the delicious homemade buttermilk biscuits covered in dark brown gravy from Sunday's pot roast.

Mother sits down across the table from me, "Is there something else bothering you today?"

She knows when I'm happy and when I'm sad. She can read my mind.

"Mrs. Bozarth made Steve sit with his feet in a garbage can because he is dirty and smelly. Then she got mad when everyone laughed at him. He is dirty and smelly, but I felt bad for him. Mrs. Bozarth scares me."

"She may be stern, but she has a reputation for being a good teacher. It is early in the year. Maybe we should give her the benefit of the doubt."

"I like her when she tells us stories about old Portland. The kids think she is strange because she saved the gate to the Portland Hotel when it was torn down to build the Meier and Frank parking lot."

"Mrs. Bozarth is a little eccentric." Mother gets up from the table and brings me a chocolate chip cookie. "Finish eating honey. It is almost time to walk back to school."

I don't want to leave the safety of the kitchen, "I wish I was more like the other kids so they wouldn't tease me."

Mother smiles, "I love you just the way you are."

YARDAGE DEPARTMENT

A gray-haired woman in sensible shoes untangles the cloth tape from the scissors dangling around her neck and measures me from shoulder to knee. "A yard and a half should do as long as you make the dress with short sleeves," she pronounces with authority gained from years of experience. My mother, an expert seamstress herself, quickly verifies the yardage and calculates the total price before she gives her consent to cut the precious fabrics. "A dress fit for a princess," someone says in passing. I'm standing with my nose just barely clearing the edge of the widest and longest table I have ever seen, while the no nonsense clerk carefully cuts the rustling turquoise taffeta and gauzy matching tulle.

It is the winter of 1954, my mother, older sister and I have made our first pilgrimage of the year to the yardage department on the 6th floor of the Meier & Frank Department Store in downtown Portland. In May or June, we will return for a few bright cottons to be made into summer tops, shorts, and pedal pushers. School shopping is next at the end of summer followed by a pattern and fabric search in November for matching Christmas dresses. We always shop at the century old department store because as my grandmother has often declared with a chuckle, "If you can't find it at Meier & Frank, you don't need it."

We start the day searching for the perfect Easter dress design in the pattern department located next to the elevators. The chairs in front of the long-slanted tables, piled high with enormous McCall's, Simplicity, and Vogue pattern books, are overflowing with mothers and daughters on the same mission. A woman behind a long counter finds our dress patterns in file drawers stuffed with the latest styles.

I stay close to my mother so I won't get lost as we move from the pattern department into the crowded rows of wooden tables covered with a profusion of color, texture and every type of fabric imaginable. The colorful feast seems to go on for miles or a least the full length of the building between SW Morrison and Alder Streets. Customers and neatly dressed sales ladies shuffle from table to table on the well-worn wooden floor. With such an abundance of choices it is hard to decide and harder yet for two girls and a mother to agree.

Finally, after my mother exercises her veto power and the fabric is cut and paid for, we walk around the escalators in the center of the building, past the bank of ornate elevators to my favorite area– Notions. Cards filled with buttons from tiny to huge, modest to ornate; zippers of every color and length; a rainbow of cotton and silk thread wound on wooden spoons; bolts of linings and inter-facings; packets of ric rac and seam binding; and coils of ribbon and trims – the abundance of choices spill out of drawers, load up the tables, hang thick on display racks, and cover every inch of wall space.

While my mother fills her list, I find myself entranced by the elegant laces, trims, and beaded decorations carefully displayed in a glass front wooden case. I am soon lost in my imagination wearing a silk satin wedding dress complete with flowing veil and shimmering tiara. Just as I start down the flower-strewn aisle, Mother gently awakens me from my daydream to tell me it is time to go home.

It should be noted here that the matching Easter dresses beau-tifully made from the taffeta and tulle we bought that day were not a big hit with my sister or me. There was an unforeseen problem reminiscent of the princess and the pea–tulle turned inside for seams is itchy.

BERRY PICKING

G randpa Roscoe could cajole anyone into or out of almost anything. While he was short on height, he was tall on energy,
enthusiasm, and charm. All he had to do to get my attention was
say, "How is my little goldie locks today?" and I was hooked.

In his customary fashion, Grandpa came by our house on a
summer evening to tempt my older sister, Judy, and me with an
"exciting" expedition to one of his farms the next morning to pick
fruit. Somewhere in the back of my mind I know I will be sorry, but
whether it is the need to feel special or sibling competition, I said
yes. "I'll come by at 6:00 to pick you up," he says as he walks back
down the driveway, straw hat in hand.

The next morning, two sleepy eyed girls fortified with a breakfast of hot Wheat Hearts and homemade cinnamon rolls are greeted
with a cheery "it's a beautiful day" as we pile into Grandpa's rickety
Ford pickup. Six years younger than my sister, I am the smallest so I
take my place in the middle of the threadbare seat wedged between
Judy, Grandpa and the tall stick shift. In that position I get the full
effect of the exhaust leaking through holes in the floorboards like
a worn out shoe.

After nearly an hour's ride, we arrive at a property close to the
Tualatin River, referred to by Grandpa as #3, to pick raspberries.
Grandpa's ten acres of prunes on a hillside above Dundee and the
five acres of filberts on Rex Hill are #1 and #2. Even an eight-
year-old can see that Grandpa's property is in no better condition
than his truck. He thinks the run down house is "fine" and the over-
grown garden has "potential." Perhaps I should also mention that
Grandpa says work is "fun."

In the cool morning air with the vines so heavy with fruit, the
job doesn't seem so big and I know the berries will be sweet to eat.
We start filling the little wooden boxes in the wooden trays held

31

around our waists with a piece of rope. At least it isn't as back-breaking as picking strawberries.

By the time I fill a couple of boxes, Grandpa has finished his first flat and Judy isn't far behind. It begins to warm up as the sun arches higher in the sky and my enthusiasm declines. The heat of the sun overhead, the intoxicating smell of the berries, and the pain in my back make me want to lie down in the tall grass and go to sleep.

Finally, with only a little help from me, the vines have given up their sweet fruit. We carefully stack the flats under a canvas tarp in the back of the truck and begin the trip back to town. It is a bit more exciting due to the downhill incline and the less than perfect brakes on the old truck. "Don't worry your mother about this," he says. I close my eyes.

Back in town, Grandpa stops by the back door of Elle's Thriftway, a neighborhood grocery store, to exchange a few flats of our freshly picked raspberries for a few crisp dollar bills.

When I return home with stained hands, scratched arms and an unsettled stomach from too many raspberries mixed with too many curves in the road, I declare, "I will never go again!" all the while knowing Grandpa's charm will make me forget my vow.

MEMORIAL DAY

D addy turns his new Mercury Montclair off of Highway 99 into a long driveway guarded by tall skinny trees spaced like soldiers along each side. Beyond the trees the grass of a large park is covered with bunches of flowers between lines of stone markers some decorated with small American flags. In the distance, a building made of pink and tan stone is also covered with flowers and flags. Cars with open trunks and open doors are parked between the trees, men and women carry armloads of flowers and vases filled with water. A few children in their Sunday best follow their parents across the grass. We have arrived at the Evergreen Memorial Park near McMinnville. Three days from today – Wednesday, May 30, 1956 – is Memorial Day. Mother told me Grandma calls the holiday "decoration day." That seems right because we are here to decorate Joe's grave. According to Daddy, "We are here to honor a fallen hero."

Mother says, "I can see the "Hanson" marker that means we're close. Look, someone is leaving. You can park in their spot." Seated in front of me, she points to a car moving out of a grassy parking place between two trees.

"It looks tight to me Beth. If I get too close to that tree it will scratch the car. There is a bigger space up ahead."

Daddy ignores Mother's protest and parks further down the road in a place big enough for two cars. All I care about is to stop moving so I can open the door and stand on solid ground. My mid-day Sunday dinner pot roast and mashed potatoes are not sure they want to stay in my stomach.

Daddy says "Judy, get out on your sister's side. I don't want you to open the door into traffic." Then he gets out from behind the steering wheel on the traffic side.

I open the door and climb down from my seat with Judy pushing from behind. Happy to be out of the car, I lean my back against the smooth green paint and shiny metal. The cool air makes my head and my stomach feel better.

"MaryLouise, don't stand against the car!"

"Oh Roland, leave her alone. Can't you see she is feeling a little car sick?" Mother comes over, touches my cheek, "Are you OK honey?"

"Better now that the car has stopped." I'm thinking about the trip back home through farmland to the Dairy Queen in Newberg, past Grandpa's prune orchard in Dundee and his nuts on Rex Hill, through the stop lights on Barber Boulevard, across the Ross Island Bridge, up Powell to 65th and into our driveway. I hope Daddy gets better at using the new power brakes.

Mother carries red and white carnations surrounded by soft fern wrapped in green waxy paper. Judy hands me the whiskbroom then picks up the grass clippers, a trowel, and a jar from the trunk. Daddy pulls out his brown leather camera bag. Similar to a line of kids in my Kindergarten, we start out to find Joe.

Judy turns to remind me in a six years older and wiser whisper, "It isn't polite to stand on dead people." I zigzag around stone markers careful not to step on the kitchen table sized space in front of them.

A few rows over from our parking place and two rows in from the drive we find Joe's flat headstone marked with a flag. Someone has already arranged red roses and purple lilacs on his grave.

Mother lays the flowers down on the grass and opens the paper. Judy takes the jar to fill it at a faucet a few rows away. Daddy trims the grass then uses the long, pointed trowel to poke around in the soft ground looking for a flower container buried by winter rains. I sweep the grass clippings from the headstone carved with a cross at the top and words Judy read to me the last time we came here.

Joseph M. McAllister
2D Lieut 571 AAF Bomb SQ
World War II
Oct 14, 1916 March 14, 1945

McAllister is Judy's last name. Joe was her daddy and my mother's first husband. He flew a big airplane in World War II that dropped bombs on Germany. A month before the end of the war another bomber ran into his plane and all except one person died. Judy was one-year-old.

Mother is sad when we come here to Joe's grave. I can tell because there is a wrinkle between her eyebrows and she has a faraway look I've seen before. Sometimes at home I see the same look when she stops in the middle of sweeping the kitchen floor and says to no one in particular, "today would be Joe's birthday." or "tomorrow would be our wedding anniversary." At times like this, she wouldn't see me if I waved my hand at her. Mother's sadness makes me feel sad.

"Beth, bring the girls over here by the flowers so I can take a picture." Daddy fusses with his light meter then sets dials on his camera. Mother, beautiful in her slim gray suit with a pale blue ruffle at the neck, and Judy, her coat open over a bright blue and orange dress, crouch down next to the flowers. Standing to the side, hands behind my back, I stare at my feet in white anklets and black patent Mary Janes. No one is smiling for Daddy's camera.

Looking back on childhood it is now clear that I was a silent and often solitary witness to my mother's grief. Because I was the recipient of her boundless love I also felt the depth of her loss. I didn't know then, but I know now that I've spent my life in search of the kind of love and friendship shared by Beth and Joe.

TEENAGE FASHION MODEL

On an August weekday morning Mother and I shop for back to school clothes at Olds & King Department Store in the Gateway shopping center east of Portland. We drive here sometimes instead of downtown because they have a huge parking lot right in front of the store. Before the beginning of each school year, we shop for one dress and one pair of sturdy shoes to last until spring. Mother sews most of my other clothes, including the baggy capris and sleeveless shirt I wear today. I started to notice that most girls' moms don't make their clothes.

While Mother looks at a sale table, I slip into the next department where a fashion model catches my attention. A tall, curvy figure in a black and white stripe swimsuit shows off everything I am not. Her black hair pulled up in a ponytail reveals gold loop earrings; red painted nails peak out of toeless high heeled shoes; painted fingernails on long graceful fingers match toes and full red lips; dark eyes look off to the side under heavy eye makeup. The model's wardrobe, displayed under clear plastic in pink boxes, could belong to Audrey Hepburn. In contrast to this stylish brunette my chunky body, cropped blond hair, homemade pedal pushers, white anklets, and Keds signal ordinary-ness not stardom. Except for her shy sideways look we have nothing in common.

The clerk notices my star struck gaze, "She was introduced last spring in New York. The clothes just came in and they are selling fast."

I run back to Mother, "I've decided what I want for my birthday next month. Come quick. You have to see."

"Slow down honey. We came here to look for a dress and shoes. The girl's department is on the other side of the store."

"It'll only take a minute." I pull on Mother's arm until she follows me.

We arrive in front of the display, "Isn't she the most beautiful thing you've ever seen? Look at these outfits." Each box holds an outfit complete with accessories. "See this one, baby dolls with a glass of milk, cinnamon roll, and diary." The cassimere coat comes with a feather decorated felt hat, a leather clutch purse and white gloves. The slinky black strapless gown dress has elbow length black gloves, a long pink chiffon scarf, glittery necklace and erring's, and a microphone on a tall stand. The wedding dress is the best. It's perfect in every tiny detail, and I picture myself in each perfect outfit.

I show Mother each costume. She gives the model a mother's look of disapproval. "This girl is pretty grown up."

"I've never seen anything like this before. None of the girls in my class have one. Please, pleeeease can this be my birthday present?

"The clothes are well made, but expensive, five dollars for the wedding dress. I could sew outfits for less. We'll see what your birthday brings.

"Don't wait too long. They might sell out." I count long narrow boxes decorated with outfits from the doll's wardrobe. How long will it take for these eleven boxes to disappear?

Every day for the next month I remind Mother about the one present I want for my ninth birthday, a Barbie doll.

SLEEPOVER

Outside everything looks perfect but there is a storm brewing. Tonight is my first slumber party. Leslie, the new girl at Kellogg this year, invited all the girls in Mrs. Collins seventh grade class to an overnight at her house. She lives three blocks away next door to the Little Green Store on 62nd and Woodward. I've stayed over at my friend Darlene's a few times, but none of the girls in my class ever invited me to a slumber party. Darlene, a year older, is bookish like me, we play Barbies together in secret, and we are the only girls in our school with braces. The mean boys call us metal mouth. Boys were not invited the party tonight.

My new round hatbox overnight bag, packed since yesterday, sits by the back door next to my favorite pillow and fat rolled up green sleeping bag lined with cozy red plaid flannel. I unzip and rezip the bag for the hundredth time to make sure every item is in place. Pink shorty pajamas, toothbrush, toothpaste, comb, a few rollers and pins for my hair, change of underwear, flashlight, diary, and my new turquoise transistor radio in a tan leather case. Mother made cookies to share with the girls.

Daddy's arrival home from work and his conversation with Mother about the stillness and strange yellow color of the sky fail to distract me. The headline on the newspaper he leaves by my feet seems like a far-off place.

I hear Mother's voice, "Mary Louise, Dinner is almost ready. You need to set the table."

We sit down to macaroni and cheese one of my favorites, but my mind distracts my stomach from the meal and the conversation between my parents about the weather.

A strong gust of wind hits the house and the lights blink. All I can think about is the slumber party.

Mother carries dishes from the table to the kitchen sink. "Oh my gosh, come and look at the cherry trees out by the street."

The surprise of Mother's outburst pulls me to the window. Cherry tree branches whip in the wind then a big gust bends the branches over like girls bent down throwing long hair over their heads.

"I can still go to the party can't I? Isn't this just a little storm? They won't cancel will they? Leslie will think I don't like her if I don't show up."

Mother places her hand on my shoulder, "I don't know honey. Maybe the wind will die down before the party starts

Daddy rushes to the window, "I'm not going out in this. Who knows what might blow down the street and hit the car."

Maybe I can walk to Leslie's. I say to myself and then another gust slaps against the house, shakes it like we are in the grip of a giant's hands.

There is a flash in the intersection of our street and Woodward. I can see wires dance there. Then the lights go out. I know this means there will be no party, and I am disappointed.

I feel around and find my overnight bag in the dark take out the flashlight and my transistor radio thinking someone on the radio will know how long this storm will last. At this point I'm not sure what upsets me more – missing my first slumber party or my fear of the wind blowing our house over. I remember the picture in the paper of the roof blown off the school. It doesn't seem so far away now.

"There is nothing to worry about. This house is as solid as they come. The shiplap under the siding is on the diagonal. No other house in the neighborhood is built that strong." Says my father.

Mother closes the venetian blinds in the living room then pulls the cord to close the drapes over a picture window the full width the sofa. "Better to cover the glass in case it breaks." As if I'm not already scared. This does it.

I curl up in the big chair with my flashlight and radio far away from the windows. Somehow the high back chair feels like a safe place. The wind is so loud now that I can't hear the radio. I take the little earpiece out of the leather case attached to the strap and place it in my ear. I roll the channel control all the way to one side until it stops then inch the dial in the other direction. Static fills my ear. Then a voice, "the wind gauge mounted on top of our roof just registered a gust of 91. We are getting reports of gusts on the Morrison Bridge of 118 mph. Let me repeat the message earlier from Mayor Terry Schrunk and the emergency broadcast. "Do not go outside under any circumstances. The worst of the storm is yet to come."

I guess that means the party has been canceled. Maybe it's better that I didn't get to Leslies before the storm. I wouldn't want to be this scared in a strange house.

A ring of the telephone makes us all jump. We thought it went off with the power. Mother finds her way to the dining room. I hear her say "Hello Mom, yes we're fine. How is everything over there? Oh know, they lost their roof? That's terrible. Then I hear Oh my gosh, Roland, MaryLouise come here quick. Look out in the back yard." All I can see are tree limbs. The whole yard is full of tree limbs. The peach tree Mother hates because it makes a mess and attracts yellow jackets is history.

Then I notice something strange. I can't hear the wind. "Is the storm over? Maybe everything is OK."

A short period of quiet is broken when another gust slams into the house. That must have been the eye of the storm, Daddy says.

The roar of a wind gust roars in my ears before it slams into the house. Like the rumble of a truck headed this way, then bam it hits. And then another and another and another. The sound of the surf, waves hitting the shore.

Good thing all my overnight gear is right here on the main floor of the house. No way am I going upstairs where the storm windows rattle and the roof creaks with each gust like the giant's fingers want to tear it off. "I'm sleeping on the floor in your bedroom," I tell Mother. I crawl into my sleeping bag, pull it up over my head and cover my ears to muffle the wail of the storm. Sometime after midnight I fall asleep thinking about a slumber party.

The next morning sun blasts in through the curtains in my parent's bedroom. No roar of wind just the buzz of chain saws.

Two weeks later at the slumber party all the girls can talk about are boys.

JUDY

I n true older sister fashion, Judy was my most faithful protector as well as my most feared adversary. She would be angry if someone was mean to me one minute and push me to tears the next. I often said I had three parents.

I've always thought Judy was jealous of me. My worst sin – I was born. She was the first grandchild and queen of the extended family for six years when I made my appearance. I'm not sure anyone asked her if she wanted a baby sister to share the attention of parents, grandparents, aunts and uncles. Add to this the fact that her father died in WWII when she was a baby. I was given preference by my father as his only child (a cause of life-long tension). It didn't help that I was cute when she was entering the awkward years before and during puberty or that I was easy going rarely causing a fuss.

Judy was never easy going. She was an energetic, inquisitive child who was difficult to keep up with especially when she was out in public. One day when she was a toddler, my mother put a harness-like tether on her to keep her from wandering off. As soon as the straps were in place, she lay down on the floor and said, "night, night." Not knowing what else to do, Mother removed the straps and Judy took off like a rocket

By the time Judy was four, she would leave the house on her own and walk several blocks to Grandma's house. She also learned to dial the phone at an early age–it is still her lifeline. In the early 1950s my parents were forced to buy a television because Judy spent all her time at friend's homes fascinated with their new TVs.

The story of Mother breaking the butter paddle when she spanked Judy is a family legend. To be honest the old wooden paddle had a crack and it is hard to imagine my mild-mannered mother hitting anyone hard enough to cause a break. Judy did put Mother's patience to the test.

My ability to pick up the skill of casual conversation was hampered by Judy's domination at the dinner table. The benefit of the situation was learning what not to do by listening to Judy talk about getting into messy situations at school, with friends, and at home. She never knew when to keep her mouth shut. I can remember suggesting I ask if we both wanted to go somewhere or do something because she was so undiplomatic. She never adopted my mother's wise old adage, "you can catch more flies with honey than with vinegar."

The age difference between us meant we didn't spend a lot of time together. No one wants their little sister around. Judy and my older cousin Mike always brought me to tears when they conspired to cut me out of the Monopoly games.

The age difference also had perks. An exciting memory from childhood is when my sister took me with her to high school football and basketball games. I felt grown up hanging out with her friends. Judy and one of her boyfriends who had a sister my age, sometimes took us with them when they went to watch fireworks or a drive-in movie. The little sisters were convenient chaperons with a boy she wasn't crazy about. Judy took me under her wing my first year at an annual conference for high school and college girls. My sister was the one who gave me a facts of life lecture – less embarrassing than talking to Mother. On my sixteenth birthday my sister decorated the dining room with streamers and handmade signs to create a special celebration.

As is usually the case with siblings, our memories of childhood events are vastly different.

On hot summer nights when I wanted her to sleep with me in the basement hide-a-bed, she usually refused because she said I was a bed hog. The way I remember it–I was willing to put up with her nighttime thrashing and clinging to my side of the bed in order to have company in the darkness of the scary basement.

A traumatic memory from early childhood of being hit in the face by a bat illustrates my point. In my version, I was the catcher standing too close to Judy as she took a swing at an incoming ball. In Judy's account, the accident was caused by a struggle between us over the bat.

She has no memory at all of her habit of turning on the overhead light late at night in our shared bedroom after I had already gone to sleep.

Judy would say she never learned to cook because our mother was afraid we would make too much mess in the kitchen. She has never forgotten or forgiven an incident when Mother returned home one afternoon to a horrible mess in the kitchen the result of her trying to fix a multi course dinner including pie on her own. I spent many hours cooking with my mother.

My sister and I had little in common except for our mother. In fact we were opposites. As we grew into adults these differences became more apparent. I'm a classic introvert requiring long stretches of solitude to process information and experiences. As is typical with extroverts, Judy thrives on conversation and is energized by being with people. I am quiet and reserved. Judy routinely tells all to anyone and everyone. I can be logical emotional and prefer, Judy seems insensitive and domineering. I am right brain, Judy is left brain. Judy is a life-long Republican; I am an Independent.

The rivalries of childhood carried into our adult years. She found a husband, Frank, who enjoys making people uncomfortable and uses Judy. They both liked to bait me – engage me in a debate about something I feel passionate about. They were a united force against me. It didn't matter what topic came up they would take the opposite view.

It was a mistake to trust my sister. I should have known better, but I wasn't thinking clearly besides she had been nicer to me lately and I was desperate for someone to talk to. Judy thought she was doing me a favor when she revealed my most private secret – she views herself as being helpful. I have never forgiven her for the heartbreaking disaster. I went to her that March day in 1977 to unload a burden and ask for a favor. I was emotionally and physically exhausted. Exhaustion from sleepless nights combined with the symptoms of mononucleosis made me feel like my body was sinking into the chair in her kitchen as if there was no bottom. Affairs and divorces were not allowed in my family.

I had known Gary since childhood. We had been good friends since college. I was miserable in a five-year marriage to "the man of my dreams." It was my husband's idea for me to have an affair with one of his best friends. He thought it would make me less boring. No one realized I would fall deeply in love. He was separated from a woman he had married out of pity and not saying no.

I couldn't have been out of her house more than an hour before she phoned my husband at the retreat center where he was attending a conference to tell him about the affair. It doesn't matter that he already knew. In fact it doesn't matter that he encouraged me to become involved with one of his best friends. What matters is I asked her not to tell ANYONE! She thought she could encourage him to fight for me. She didn't know he didn't care.

Then she told my parents. They didn't know and they didn't need to know. The result was tragic. I didn't find out until years later (Gary never said a word he just disappeared. Roland went unannounced to Gary's workplace and demanded he stay away from me.)

When she has power over me she uses it. In her mind she is just helping. A life threatening illness discovered about ten years ago has mellowed Judy somewhat. Still a loyal Republican and a Conservative, she supported Obama. I was shocked when they told me they registered voters for the campaign.

FACTS OF LIFE

"Yuk! I'm never going to let a boy stick his thing in me." I fidget in my desk chair across from my sister Judy in the little room we use as a study, "Is that what they mean when they say she went all the way?"

Judy is six years older. She knows about these things. She is engaged. "Yeah, girls have to be careful not to excite boys with too many kisses. Sometimes Frank says he has to take me home because he needs to settle down."

I stare through crisscross curtains over double hung windows at the outline of tree-covered Mt. Tabor Park. On Friday and Saturday nights the roads up there are lined with cars. This must be why the windows are steamed.

I want to know and I don't want to know. "Do you have to take your clothes off?"

"Well yeah mostly."

"Naked with a boy? He sees me, I see him?"

"Sometimes it's dark."

"No way!"

"It will be different when you fall in love."

I don't have to worry yet. Boys don't notice me. I'm flat chested and awkward. Until eighth grade last year, I still wore anklets and little girl dresses.

This *facts of life* discussion with Judy comes a few days after I asked Mother how God knows when to give a woman a baby. They showed us a filmstrip about girl's bodies and boy's bodies in seventh grade home economics, but failed to talk about how the two bodies fit together and what happens when they do. Now that I know I can't imagine why there are any babies at all. Happily ever after romantic novels and crushes from a distance are enough for me.

Mother and Daddy went on a Sunday drive this afternoon leaving us alone for the "talk." I guess they thought it would be easier for Judy to tell me. I can see that she relishes her grown up sister role.

"Mother's mother never told her anything about sex. She learned what she needed to know from my daddy on their wedding night."

I imagine our mother and Judy's father Joe, the kind looking man in the photograph that used to hang on the wall in this room. "I guess since you're here they figured out what to do. Mother and my Daddy must have done it at least once to make me."

Judy rolls her eyes, "Married people don't do this once and not just to make babies."

I refuse to picture my parents doing what Judy just told me. "I don't want to know any more."

She barges ahead anyway, "Do you remember when Mother went to the hospital when you were in Brownies?"

"Yeah, she missed my Fly-Up from Brownie to Girl Scout."

"She had to go to the hospital because she had a miscarriage. She was going to have a baby and then she wasn't. So that means they did it at least twice."

"You mean I almost had a brother or sister? How come no one ever told me?"

"People don't talk about that sort of thing with little kids." Judy straightens up. She flashes an older, smarter sister look that silences me.

"Let's get back to talking about what happens when a boy is too excited. Do you remember Sarah, the young woman at church who was in charge of the Sunday school?"

"You mean the one who left because she had to go to the hospital to have a tumor removed? The kids thought she looked funny when her stomach got so big it pushed up her belt.

"It wasn't a tumor, it was a baby. Her boyfriend, a seminary student, got her pregnant. They just told that story about the tumor so kids wouldn't ask questions."

"So, that's why Sarah disappeared. She was there one Sunday and gone the next. Not even a goodbye. We thought she didn't like us."

Judy's patience is on empty, "Don't change the subject again. I just want you to know that you need to be careful even with a seminary student."

"Don't worry, the whole idea of being naked with a boy disgusts me."

46

GLORIA LAVONNE

Two black and white photographs of a young woman are displayed next to each other inside the white paper folder I hold in my hand. The young woman in the photo on the left faces the camera arms at her sides in an awkward pose. Long bangs meet thick eyebrows, her face squared off by a wide below-the-ear hairstyle. The pose, camera angle, unflattering light, white sleeveless A-line dress, and chunky white patent shoes make her look overweight and uneasy.

The young woman in the other photograph is turned to the side, white gloved hands on her hips, elbows bent, one foot extended with a slight turn of the ankle in a model's pose. Wearing a dark short sleeve straight shift, slim pointed heals, narrow brows, and short cropped hair under a white straw pillbox hat – this fashionable young woman exudes confidence.

Two photos, one young women, one smile…my smile. The folder in my hand is proof that *"Mary Louise Ott has successfully completed the Gloria La Vonne Training in Professional Finishing and Fashion and is so honored with this Certificate of Accomplishment. Received August 4, 1967 from Gloria LaVonne Finishing and Modeling School – A Success School for Women."*

Although the *"Before Training"* and *"After Training"* photographs where posed to maximize the contrast, no camera can capture the dramatic transformation of my self-image over the past six weeks. More than ten pounds overweight, clueless about hair, makeup or fashion, uneasy in my own body and uncomfortable around anyone except my family – no one needed finishing more than this six-teen-year-old. Bless my mother for making it possible.

Mother doesn't wear much makeup and isn't into fashion. She is beautiful just the way she is and has confidence to spare. My shyness is a worry to her and a handicap for me as I start my last year of high school in September. Mother is always looking for opportunities to help build my self-esteem. An advertisement in the Oregonian may have captured her attention:

"Parents…
Can you Think of One Gift that would mean
more to your daughter than
a GIFT CERTIFICATE to Gloria LaVonne Finishing &
Modeling School?
A Lifetime of Beauty, Poise and Self-Confidence
Call Now

I could see satisfaction in Mother's eyes today when she sat up front at the fashion show we staged to celebrate graduation from training. I'm proud of what I have accomplished in the last six weeks even though some of the ideas were strange such as telling us to shave our arms as well as our legs. Too hairy or not, the fuzz on my arms stays.

They taught us to walk with a book on our head just like on TV or in the movies. According to our teacher, Miss Jackie, we should, "push off with our toes and glide across the floor. Don't bounce like a bunny. Imagine your body pulled up by a rope attached to the top of your head." I also learned how to dress and what colors to wear, "Your basic dress should be navy blue, not black. The color should complement rather than overwhelm your porcelain skin and strawberry blond hair." A professional styled my hair and taught me to use makeup, "subtle use of line and color on the eye and just a touch of pink on the cheek highlights your assets without looking like a clown. A short hairstyle flatters your oval face."

Today I am pleased with my accomplishment, but six weeks ago on the first day of training in June, transformation seemed impossible.

The first morning of finishing school Mother drove me downtown to ease my anxiety. "I hope your morning goes well honey. You can tell me all about it this afternoon. Do you remember where to catch the bus?"

"Yes, over by Meier & Frank. Daddy said the Division and Powell buses both stop there." Except for school and holiday shopping, I don't travel down town. Taking the bus alone is rare. Every week day for the next six weeks I will make the trip to town for my class from nine until noon by myself. After class, maybe I will have time to explore the ten floors of Meier & Frank Department Store, Lipman's across the street, Charles F. Berg on Broadway, and Nordstrom Shoes a block away.

I say goodbye to Mother and climb worn wooden steps to the mezzanine of the Woodlark Building on SW Alder. A friendly receptionist greets me and directs me to a large room with a platform at one end and chairs around the walls. A few girls are chatting together. I sit on the opposite side of the room by myself. By nine o'clock, fifteen girls of all shapes and sizes fill most of the chairs.

A tall middle-aged woman dressed in a slim sapphire suit with matching belt and soft cream colored scarf at the neck swoops into the room. A gold bracelet decorates one arm and large pearl earrings are clipped to her ears. Her blonde hair is swept up into a French roll. Her face looks like a movie star I've seen on the cover of a magazine. Everything about her appearance and manner is perfect.

"Good morning young ladies. I am Miss LaVonne director of this school. Welcome to an unforgettable experience that will build your poise and confidence." Her piercing eyes circle the room then she continues, "In the next six weeks you will learn how to walk and choose clothes to flatter your figure and coloring. We will show you how to apply subtle makeup and style your hair to compliment the shape of your face. Specialists will teach you about nutrition and exercise to keep your body fit. With this knowledge you will forget about yourself. There will be no need for self-consciousness. You will gain the polished look you envy in others."

I look at Miss LaVonne and then the girls in the room. We have a long way to go. Right now being here in the presence of someone as perfect as Miss LaVonne makes me MORE self-conscious.

"Now please welcome your teacher for the next six weeks, Miss Jackie." A beautiful young woman steps forward and walks across the room as though she is floating. Miss Jackie's silky black shoulder length hair is styled in a below the ear flip accented by a black headband. She wears a black dress, short turquoise jacket and black heals.

Small gold hoop erring's, her only jewelry. Miss Jackie's smile lights up the room. I feel less intimidated.

"Now young ladies, I will leave you in Miss Jackie's capable hands." Miss LaVonne sweeps out of the room.

"Good morning girls. I'm excited to be here with you today. Before today's lesson on how to sit, stand, and walk, our first task is to pose for the photographer."

YOUNG ADULT
AND ADULTHOOD

1965 – My First Love, Michael

1971 – Married Michael

1976 and 1977 – Love Affair with Gary Howarth

1978 – Divorced Michael

1981 – Married Richard Katz

1981 – Birth of My Son with Richard Katz

1984 – Gary's Son Gary Howarth ll was Born

1989 – Birth of My Daughter with Richard Katz

1996 – Love Affair with Gary Howarth

1996 – Divorced Richard Katz

1996 – Married Gary Howarth

FIRST DATE — MIKE

My skin, exposed between white knee socks and Pendleton wool plaid Bermuda shorts, is pink and tingles from the cold. Fashion trumps function for this style conscious seventeen-year-old. The street light in front of Dick's house illuminates a quiet snow covered scene. A fog of warm breath meets below freezing air. We are laughing, throwing snow, and talking about nothing of consequence. A few years ago, I would never imagine having fun with Dick, formerly known as Dickey the one year older neighbor boy who hid my bat in the bushes, taunted me when I played in the front yard, and unscrewed Christmas lights to irritate my father. Things changed last year when I helped him pass chemistry.

Boys started to notice me after I completed the *Gloria LaVonne Finishing and Modeling School* course last summer. The shy, frumpy "A" student has a whole new look and more confidence to match. Although I enjoy the attention, not all the boys interest me. For example, Don doesn't count as a boyfriend prospect because I know him too well. His family has been friends with mine since before either of us was born. I'm not happy about a tiny Christmas package from him lurking under our tree.

My good friend Gary is a year older and cute, but he is too tall. His six foot seven makes me look like a shrimp at five foot three. The biggest problem is Gary acts crazy when he is with the Don. Last spring on the beach trip, Don thought it was funny when Gary threw a sand-covered water balloon in my face.

My first official date with a boy was last weekend. I met Ron on a backpacking trip at the end of the summer where we talked for hours about the meaning of life under the stars on the High Divide Trail in the Olympic National Park. He took me to the Benson High School Christmas dance last Saturday night and we have a date next week to see *Gone with the Wind*. The only disadvantage – he is a year younger and doesn't have a license so his mom drives.

The real prize is Mike Small. I decided to marry him when I was a freshman. He doesn't know it yet.

The snow throwing game is interrupted by my mother's voice calling from our driveway across the street, "Mary Louise, telephone for you."

"Who is it?" I mouth the words as I enter the warm kitchen through the back door.

Mother whispers back, "A boy."

Exhilarated from the cold and the prospect of a phone call from a boy, I pick up the heavy black receiver from the phone stand in the corner of the dining room, "Hello."

"Hi, this is Mike Small. Your mom said you were out playing in the snow."

My stomach does a flip – Mike Small is on the other end of the phone. I must keep cool and not let my voice give away too much excitement, "The snow is so beautiful. They say we may have a white Christmas."

"Maybe, I can't remember ever having one. It's supposed to warm up in a couple of days." Mike pauses, "I was wondering if you would like to go with me to see *Gone with the Wind* next week on Thursday the 28th? They've re-issued the film in wide screen and stereo sound. It's playing at *The Broadway* downtown."

Of course, I want to go. My brain whizzes through potential complications. When is my date with Ron for the same movie? Mike could have picked any film playing in downtown Portland from *The Jungle Book* to *Camelot*, *Wait Until Dark*, or even *Valley of the Dolls* although my parents would disapprove of the last one. A first date with Mike is all that matters. Who cares about the movie or if I will see it twice.

"That sounds like fun, I just read *Gone with the Wind* and would love to see the movie." I hope he can't hear nervousness in my voice.

"Great, the evening show starts at eight. Is it OK to pick you up at 7:15? Parking might be difficult to find downtown."

"Perfect, I'll be ready at 7:15."

We say goodbye and that's all there is to it. Mike Small has asked me out for a date. I hang up the phone and start dancing my way around the dining room. All thoughts of other boys blow away with the snowflakes outside the window. I've been waiting for this call for three years. December 19, 1967, my lucky day.

It was at the high school youth group beach trip four years ago when I decided Mike was an ideal candidate for marriage. Mike was nothing like my short, balding, mechanical engineer father. He was a junior – two years ahead of me in school and three years older – tall, but not too tall, handsome with brown eyes and dark hair. His long arms, big hands, and size fifteen feet gave him an endearing boyish awkwardness. Now he is a mature college man. In my imagination Mike is my Joe, Mother's beloved first husband, making him the perfect prince for my happily-ever-after fantasy. The clincher is that Mike plans to attend seminary after he graduates from Lewis and Clark College. I could be a preacher's wife like my grandmother.

For three year's I was invisible. An older girl named Janet pursued and captured Mike. I hated her. Everything changed this summer–thank you Gloria LaVonne! In September he started to sit across the aisle from mother and me at the eleven-o-clock service on Sunday morning providing weekly opportunities to flirt as we leave our seats at the end.

After three months of flirting, I took a big chance and sent him a card for his 20th birthday on December 12th. A few days later I received a Christmas card signed "Best Regards, Mike." Last Sunday after the choir Christmas concert, I invited Mike and Gary to carol with the youth group. Mike asked my friend Bernice and me to ride in his car. I grabbed the seat across from him at the chili dinner afterward.

Mother's voice brings me back to reality, "Don't you have a date with Ron next week? Isn't it for the same movie?"

I go to the calendar to check the dates. "Ron is next Wednesday the 27th, Mike asked me for the 28th. It should be OK as long as neither one finds out, especially not Mike."

The snow cancels school giving me an early holiday and more time to daydream. I can hardly wait until I see Mike on Sunday. At the morning service he sits next to my mother and hangs around longer than usual after the service. That evening at the Christmas Eve service I am a candle lighter so I can't sit near Mike. After the service he touches my arm and wishes me a Merry Christmas. On the other side of the sanctuary Don and Gary are whispering to each other. I'm flying too high to give them much notice.

Christmas day I find a single pearl necklace in the package under the tree from Don exactly like the single pearl necklace from my parents except Don's is on a silver chain and theirs is gold. If I wear that silver chain around my neck, I have to be nice to him. I like him as a friend, not a boyfriend.

Mother reminds me, "You need to call Don and thank him for the necklace."

"Do I have to? I don't want to encourage him."

"Yes, you have to. You might as well do it now and get it over with."

Don answers the phone, I thank him and I'm ready to hang up when he says, "Mike knows you have a date to the same movie the night before your date with him."

My heart sinks to my toes, "How do you know?"

"Gary told me."

"How does Gary know?"

"Don't you know he lives with Mike's family? Maybe it just came up when they were talking."

"Yes Don, I know Gary lives with the Smalls. How did Mike find out about the date?"

"Everyone knows," Don's voice has a pleased-with-himself lilt.

I hang up the phone. The news couldn't be worse. So that's what Don and Gary were up to last night. Those two! How did everyone find out? I didn't tell anyone. Don's mom always seems to know all the gossip. Maybe she is involved.

I spend the rest of the day in a fit of anxiety unable to sit still or join in the celebration around me. I consider methods of torture for both Don and Gary. Mother says she thinks Don just made it all up. I hope she is right.

Two days later the Wednesday night date with Ron is a pleasant dress rehearsal for the main event to follow on Thursday. When I don't think about Mike, I enjoy going out with Ron even though it is a drag to have his mother drive. A flutter ripples through my body when he holds my hand in the back seat of the car. The rough texture of his tweed wool sports coat against my skin combined with the earthy scent of English Leather cologne thrills my senses. If his mom wasn't eying us through the rear-view mirror, I could snuggle up here all night. Thoughts about Mike take over as soon as the back door closes and Ron walks down the driveway to his mother's car.

Preparation for my date with Mike starts early the next morning when I wash my hair and put it up on rollers. To make sure it is dry in time I sit with my head inside a blue plastic cap attached by a long hose to a noisy hair drier blowing air so hot my face turns red. After the drier I try different outfits settling on a slim fitting blood-red wool dress Mother made from a Vogue Couturier pattern.

Before dinner I soak in the tub for a half hour dreaming about my life as Mrs. Mike Small. After the bath, I dust myself lightly with Estee Lauder Youth Dew powder, slip a robe over a lacy slip, and comb out my hair. When every blonde hair is ratted and coaxed into an understated bouffant shape I spritz on enough hair spray to hold in a wind tunnel. A thin line of eyeliner, a hint of blue gray shadow to compliment my blue eyes, and just enough mascara to darken blonde lashes–Gloria LaVonne would be proud.

I pick at my dinner without eating more than a few bites then I wiggle into a panty girdle, fasten the tops of a new pair of hose into the clips, and step into the stylish dress. The last touch is a meticulous application of lipstick with a tiny brush. I'm ready and it is only 6:45.

Butterflies are playing with the scraps of dinner in my stomach. I turn on the front porch light then pace from the kitchen to the living room and back again several times. On one turn through the kitchen, Mother asks me to dry the dishes and attempts to calm me with light conversation.

Mother's words float around the room without registering in my brain until I hear; "Joe took me to see *Gone with the Wind* when it first came out."

My dishtowel stops in mid-air, "Did you just say you went to this movie with Joe?"

"Yes, it opened in 1939 the year we were married. I was nineteen."

I think about my happily-ever-after fantasy and wonder to myself, was Mike's selection of movie a coincidence or preordained?

My position in front of the kitchen window facing the street makes it possible to dry dishes and scan for car lights at the same time. Lights come and go. No one stops. The dishes are dry, the kitchen tidy, and the garbage out. At last, car lights stop at the curb – my prince has arrived in his mother's dark blue early sixties Valiant. I back away from the window to avoid detection.

The bell rings. Mother scurries into the living room to answer the door. From a safe place between the kitchen and living room, I peak at the reflection of the front door in a mirror above the fireplace. The door opens, there is Mike Small standing on my porch dressed in a navy blue suit, white shirt, and striped tie. In *Gone with the Wind*, Scarlett O'Hara would swoon at the sight. I attempt to compose myself then slip out of the room before he sees me.

"Good evening Mrs. Ott."

"Come in out of the cold Mike." Mother shakes his hand and closes the door, "Mary Louise, Mike is here."

This should be my cue to enter, but my feet are stuck. I feel awkward now that he is here – what do I talk about? I take a deep breath and think *poise*…"Hello Mike, I'm ready to go except for my coat."

"Nice to see you Mary Louise." Mike gives me what might be an approving glance then turns to my mother, "I hope you know that *Gone with the Wind* is almost four hours long. We might not be back until well after midnight."

Mother doesn't let on that she engaged in the same conversation with Ron last night, "Thank you for saying something. The late hour isn't a problem. I hope you enjoy your evening."

Mike helps me with my camel hair coat, offers me his arm, escorts me down the driveway to the car, we are on our way.

We park a short distance from SW Broadway where blazing marquees light the street with Hollywood magic starting at the *Orpheum, Fox* and *Music Box* theatres and ending with the elegant *Paramount* where *Camelot* is playing. Across the street is *The Broadway Theater*, a block long flashy art deco gem built in the 1920s. The wrap around marquee displays *Gone with the Wind* in huge letters. The lights are brighter than last night, the crowd more animated, my heart beats faster.

We walk under lights more brilliant than day, pass a ticket taker who – thank goodness – doesn't remember me, enter the glitzy lobby, and find our seats in an impressive hall that is beginning to feel it's age. I don't care if I saw this four-hour movie twenty-four hours ago and Mike doesn't say a word about my other date. I rest my left arm on the velvet armrest a fraction of an inch away from the smooth sleeve of Mike's suit coat. He shifts in his seat closing the gap. The light touch of his sleeve is as intoxicating as a full embrace. The lights dim, the drama begins.

Two hours pass. Deep red sky behind Tara fades leaving Scarlett's life in shambles until after intermission.

Mike asks, "Would you like to get some popcorn and go outside for a few minutes? We still have a lot of movie to watch. A break will help."

The crowd pushes us into the lobby and then out under the marquee. I launch into a discussion about the movie because no other topic of conversation enters my romance-addled brain, "It seems like Scarlett is out of touch with reality. I don't understand why she is so set on Ashley – he has no backbone and is too self-absorbed. I'm rooting for Rhett – he isn't as much of rouge as he pretends. He saves Scarlett more than once."

"Don't tell me too much. I haven't read the book." Mike changes the conversation to tales about his job as a DJ at KLCC, the Lewis and Clark College radio station. I hang on every word.

An usher calls us back for part two. We flow with the crowd into the theater.

It is after midnight when Mike drives me home. He escorts me to the back door where he bends down to brush his lips against my cheek. We say goodnight then he walks back down the driveway to the car.

Mike's car lights disappear leaving the street dark. The evening is a dream and like a dream only fragments of memory remain. Was that a kiss? I want more.

Days pass, New Year's Eve is over, the Christmas tree comes down, school starts, homework piles on – I may die waiting for a phone call and another date with Mike.

BUDDING ROMANCE

I close my eyes and twist the stem of an apple, "Will Mike call, won't Mike call? Will Mike call, won't Mike call? Will Mike call?" The stem breaks.

My lunch buddy Debbie laughs, "You gave the stem a little help."

"No I didn't. The stem doesn't lie."

It's the first week of January. We are eating lunch at the "uncool" end of the "cool" table in the basement cafeteria at Franklin High School. Three eight-foot tables pushed together end-to-end put us at least twenty feet away from cool. We are tolerated here because we are seniors and because I'm the yearbook editor. Better stay on the good side of the yearbook editor. Girls at the cool end of the table are members of the right clubs, cheer on the rally squad, and hold class offices. Cool girls never bring a homemade lunch and none of them ever sit down to eat. They hover around the end of the table eating pizza and flirting with the boys swarming at their own cool table nearby.

Debbie and I have been eating lunch together since we met in senior English at the beginning of the school year and found we share common interests. We are both planning to go to college and studies matter more to us than parties. Neither one of us has ever been part of the cool crowd. The first three years of high school I ate lunch with the nerds in the basement lunchroom across the courtyard from here. Like me the nerds bring their lunch. Mother packs mine in a brown paper bag. Today's lunch is a tuna sandwich on a homemade roll, two homemade chocolate chip cookies, and an apple. I crunch into the stem-less apple. An avalanche of laughter rushes down on us from the other end of the table. The cool girls are preening and prancing.

"I bet none of them have college boyfriends."

"Neither do you. At least not unless Mike calls you for another date."

Debbie is right. It has been more than a week since our first date to see *Gone with the Wind*. Maybe tonight.

The next day my excitement threatens to burst before lunch. When the bell rings, I sprint to my locker and then down the stairs to the cafeteria. "Hey Debbie, the apple twist worked. Michael called last night. He asked me to go with him to see *Camelot*. It's playing at the Paramount downtown."

"Michael? I thought his name was Mike."

"Mike is short for Michael. His family calls him Michael. I decided last night the longer version sounds more sophisticated."

"So, when is your date with Michael?" She sounds out the name, laughs then rolls her eyes.

"Saturday night. I can't wait." Thoughts about the movie and what dress to wear fill my mind. I'm Guinevere to Michael's Lancelot. I imagine myself sitting in the elegant Paramount Theater with our hands touching while the lovers kiss on screen. Maybe he'll give me a real kiss this time. Nothing penetrates my thoughts, not Debbie, not the cafeteria noise, not the smell of pizza or fish sticks, not even the laughter of the cool girls. I have another date with Michael Small. Will I be pretty enough, witty enough, worthy enough to keep him as a boyfriend?

Monday lunch Debbie is waiting for me at my locker, "How was the date? Did he kiss you?"

"Maybe." Heat starts to flow up my face.

"Oh my, I can see by the blush and the silly smile that he did. I want all the details at lunch." She drags me by the arm down the cafeteria steps. We take our usual seats at the long table and pull out our homemade lunches.

"OK, I'm ready." Debbie's eyes are glued to me. She won't give up until I spill the whole story. I've never had anything this private to tell her. I'm eager to share and embarrassed at the same time.

"The whole evening was dreamy. This time he gave me a real kiss on the lips. It didn't last long. He walked me to the back door, kissed me and said goodbye so fast I almost didn't think it happened."

"A kiss on the lips is progress." Debbie takes a bite of her sandwich and continues to grill me. "Did you go out after the movie?"

"*Camelot* was shorter than *Gone with the Wind*. We had time to go to Roses' Delicatessen and share one of those huge pieces of German Chocolate cake. He told me more about his classes at college. He studies Greek."

"Greek? He must be smart."

"Michael said he has to take Greek and Hebrew because he is going to seminary after graduation."

"Did he say anything about another date?"

"He wants to show me the Lewis and Clark College campus and the radio station."

"I guess its official ML. You have a college boyfriend. This is almost as good as having one myself."

It's the end of February. Debbie has been following the progress of my relationship with Michael as though watching a lunchtime soap opera. Kisses and handholding are on the top of Debbie's list of interests, but those aren't the only topics we talk about. I tell her about Michael's phone calls several times a week and what he says when he sits next to me at church every Sunday. Last week she wanted to know all about the visit to the college radio station. This week I told her Michael's mom invited me for dinner.

Debbie is waiting for me in the cafeteria eager for the next episode, "Is the big *meet the family* dinner tomorrow night?"

"Yes, I'm nervous about meeting Michael's mom."

"Don't you know his family from church?"

"Not well. His twin sister Mary is a junior at Oregon State. She was chatty and pleasant the only time I met her, but I don't know if she will be home this weekend. His sister Linda is in her first year studying trombone at the New England Conservatory of Music in Boston. I'm relieved that she won't be there. She is the family prodigy." I push my nose up with my index finger to make a point. "From what Michael has told me, his little sister Dee Dee is a bit of a pain. I don't know much about his mom except that when my mother called on Mrs. Small after her husband died she barely spoke and seemed irritated by the visit. The only thing that saved Mother was Michael's grandmother, Mrs. Kingston. She was friendly."

"I can see why you would be nervous. Maybe the grandmother will show up. I expect the whole story on Monday."

The dinner is tonight. I'm in Michael's car on the way to his house. My stomach, unsettled by nerves, is queasy. The drive gives me plenty of time to spin every possible disaster through my mind. It takes thirty minutes to drive from my home in Southeast Portland to his house in a Northeast neighborhood located between the expensive houses on Alameda Ridge and the dilapidated houses below. His family moved here from Seattle four years ago after his dad died of a brain tumor. Originally from Portland, the family followed Mr. Small around the country when he was in the Coast Guard.

"Michael breaks the silence in the car. I hope you aren't nervous about meeting my family? Mary is home for the weekend and you'll have a chance to meet Grandma Kingston tonight. She is coming over after work."

Maybe Mary and Mrs. Kingston will save me.

Michael drives into the garage under the house. He helps me out of the car and we walk through the damp unfinished basement to the steps. The door on the landing at the top opens into a dimly lit kitchen with walls in need of a new coat of paint and a gold carpet in need of cleaning. A table, covered with playing cards laid out for some kind of card game, sits in a niche off to one side. Water boiling in a pan on the stove steams the windows. The acrid smell of broccoli hits my nose. My sensitive stomach quivers at the thought of eating a vegetable with such a nasty odor.

"Hello Mary Louise." Michael's mom looks at me then back to the lumpy brown sauce she is stirring. Dressed in a geometric patterned blouse and gray polyester pants, her features are sharp, her eyes deep set behind black-rimmed glasses.

"It was nice of you to invite me for dinner Mrs. Small."

Mary looks up from behind the refrigerator door. "Hi Mary Louise, good to see you again." She carries a head of lettuce from the refrigerator to the sink. Mary walks with a slight limp. Michael told me her limp was caused by an injury at birth. He joked that it came from a kick he gave her on the way out. His mother cried all night after the December day in 1947 she was told to expect twins.

Her husband was away in the merchant marines. Mary first then Michael arrived the next day two months early.

Mrs. Small stops stirring, "Yes, we are happy to have you over for dinner. Michael, show Mary Louise around while we wait for your grandmother."

"I'll take your coat and give you a tour." Michael drapes my coat over a kitchen chair piled with books.

In the dining room the table is set for six. Glass front cupboards on each side of a built in buffet are filled with a jumble of glassware and dishes. The top of the buffet is clear except for a vase filled with plastic flowers. I wonder if it was tidied for my visit.

Michael's eight-year-old sister, Dee Dee, is sprawled with her legs spread in an unladylike position on a long slipcovered sofa in the living room watching TV. She has not outgrown what my grandmother calls baby fat. Her shoulder length hair defies the yellow headband meant to bring order. "Hi Dee Dee, this is Mary Louise." She ignores us. "Dee Dee is short for Anna Dee. She was named after my grandmother."

We cross the entry hall to the den. "Did Gary tell you about scaring him one night last week when he came home late from work?"

"No, I haven't talked to Gary since Christmas." I'm not going to tell Michael that I don't plan to talk to Gary any time soon. I haven't forgiven him or Don for their attempt to sabotage my first date with Michael.

"I have to tell you this great story about Gary. It was after midnight when I heard him drive up and park at the curb. He uses this outside entrance to the den when it's late because we leave the door unlocked. I crept down here and stood like this." Michael stands with his back against the wall next to the hinge side of the door. "Gary came through the door. He was standing in front of me facing the other direction when he pushed the door closed. I reached out and placed my hand on his shoulder. His knees went weak and he let out a squeal like a cat. It's easy and fun to scare Gary." After what Gary and Don did at Christmas, I don't have a lot of sympathy. I join Michael in a laugh at Gary's expense.

"I'll show you my room upstairs." We pass the bathroom. Next to it the master bedroom door is ajar. Through the narrow opening I notice the bed is unmade and littered with clothes.

Piles of books and papers fill the corners of uncarpeted stairs. We turn left into the wood paneled hall at the top. A door at the end of the hall stands open. "Mary and Linda sleep in this room when they are home."

Michael points to a room across the hall. "Over here is the room I share with Gary. He's at work so he won't be here for dinner." A cluttered desk is centered in front of a pair of double hung windows. There is just enough space on each side for extra-long twin sized beds. Michael picks up a fat envelope full of photos and plops down on the bed. "I want to show you these black and white photographs I took on a hike last summer. Sit here." He pats the blanket. The sag in the mattress presses us together. Is it proper to be alone in a boy's bedroom?

Mary calls from the bottom of the stairs, "Dinner is ready."

Back in the dining room, Michael's grandmother has arrived.

"Mary Louise this is my grandmother Mrs. Kingston."

"I'm happy to meet you Mary Louise." Mrs. Kingston has a grandmotherly look about her. White hair, a soft body that jiggles when she walks, her eyes twinkle as though she just thought of something interesting or funny. She reaches out toward me, wraps her arms and her spicy perfume around me in a wholehearted squeeze.

This is a greeting I understand. I come from a family of huggers. "I'm happy to meet you too, Mrs. Kingston." If she only knew how happy.

We take our seats. Michael is on my right at one end of the table. His mom sits at the other. Dee Dee on my left, Mrs. Kingston across from me, and Mary between her mother and grandmother. We bow our heads while Michael, the man of the family and the future seminary student, blesses the food.

Michael is different from my father in every way. At home Daddy would have started the meal with a prayer as long as a sermon. Daddy is short, stocky, and bald. Michael is six foot two, muscular, his dark brown hair thick enough to last into old age. Michael has a sense of humor and talks about interesting topics such as photography and music as well as his liberal ideas about politics and social issues. Daddy's favorite topics are religion, dissertations on his latest inventions, and criticism of Democrats, civil rights marchers, and anti-war demonstrators. Daddy says, "At least the boy is clean cut, not like those dirty hippies." Michael is solid and serious about his future, but he also likes to have fun. My father is just serious.

Mrs. Small passes the food. I dish up a small serving of stroganoff and noodles, two flowerets of limp broccoli and some salad. Despite my dislike of broccoli, I eat it to keep from embarrassing myself in front of Michael's family.

I'm chewing a bite of stroganoff hoping to settle the broccoli in my stomach when Michael asks his mom, "Did you use bear meat in the stroganoff this time?" He looks my way for a reaction and laughs. "Just kidding." Sometimes Grandma Kingston's friend Harvey brings us bear meat.

Mrs. Kingston gives Michael a stern look then turns to me, "Don't let him tease you Mary Louise. He is quite the practical joker."

"Bear meat is a treat and so are the huckleberries we pick with Harvey. The real feast is when he takes us clamming on the Washington Coast. There is nothing finer than clams fried in egg and cracker crumbs." Michael looks like he just tasted something delicious in his mind.

"I've never eaten huckleberries. Aren't they sour?" I focus on the berries because I can't think about how much I don't want to eat bear meat or fried clams.

"Not the berries Harvey finds at Indian Heaven near Mt. Adams. They are sweet and plump. I use them in pies. Maybe you can go with us at the end of the summer when the berries are ripe." Mrs. Kingston's eyes penetrate my defenses. She flashes a reassuring smile my way as though she sees the discomfort I'm trying to hide. Then she changes the subject. "Speaking of summer, Michael said you will be going on a trip to Europe."

"Yes, it's a ten-week study tour of London and nine cities on the continent including Paris, Berlin, Warsaw, and Rome. This term I'm taking a night class on British culture and history at Portland State. I've been preparing for the trip since I was accepted in December. The shots are the worst part."

Mrs. Small joins the conversation. "When do you leave?"

"In June, a couple weeks after graduation."

"Michael will have a lonely summer." Mrs. Kingston winks at her grandson, "They say absence makes the heart grow fonder."

While I hope that is true, I ignore her last comment to neutralize the blush rushing up my neck. "At an orientation meeting in April, we will each be given a rucksack to carry our belongings instead of a suitcase."

"Hmm, ten weeks living out of a ruck sack. I can picture a line of disheveled students weighed down with overstuffed sacks on their backs trouping through the streets of Paris." Mrs. Small's face softens as the image provokes a chuckle around the table.

While Michael's mother is less friendly than Mrs. Kingston she is not as scary as expected. I survive the remainder of the meal, the conversation, the dinner cleanup, and my first game of Hearts. Everyone at the table including Michael's mom, helps me learn the game. My family doesn't play cards. At one time they considered it sinful. How can a game called Hearts be sinful?

It's after midnight by the time Michael drives me home. The end of a date is my favorite part. Not just because we kiss. At the end of a date Michael parks the car in front of my house and we have time to talk without anyone else around. He slides his arm around my shoulders, pulls me close to the warmth of his body. I'm a character in a Jane Austin novel. I feel safe and special. I feel loved.

"How was Saturday night? Is his mom as scary as you thought?" Debbie stares at me in anticipation of the latest report.

"No, not scary just quiet. Mrs. Kingston and Mary did most of the talking. Michael's grandmother invited me to a Buckaroo game. She has three tickets."

"Isn't that ice hockey? Don't they have big fights at those games?" Debbie wrinkles her face into a look of disgust.

"Fights? Oh, I hope not. Michael and his grandmother said the games are fast and exciting. They have a great time together. If Michael and his grandmother enjoy ice hockey, so will I."

Debbie face relaxes, "I guess a date is a date."

March and April disappear in a flurry of homework, tryouts for commencement speaker, preparation for my trip, and dates with

Michael. His grandmother takes us to Buckaroo playoff games. It's hard not to get caught up in the excitement even though ice hockey isn't my favorite pastime. I don't cheer the fights. When the player's boxes on both sides of the rink empty onto the ice the brawl delays the game. Fights make us late. Fights cut into cuddle time at the end of a date.

May is consumed with thoughts about showing Michael off at the senior prom. The night of the dance I dress like a princess in the sky-blue brocade, floor-length gown Mother and I sewed from a Vogue Couturier pattern designed by Bellville Sassoon of London. Michael and I stand side-by-side in a spotlight at the top of the new Hilton Hotel ballroom steps. My above the elbow white gloved arm rests on the sleeve of Michael's pale blue dinner jacket. The student body president announces us to oohs and ahs from my friends and looks of surprise from the cool girls. It doesn't even matter that we don't know how to dance.

Between the prom and graduation, I practice reciting Frost's poem *The Road Not Taken* for my graduation speech, finish senior projects, and pile clothes, film, writing paper, and other essentials next to the gray rucksack I will carry all summer. I bounce between anticipation and apprehension. Will I survive ten weeks away from Michael?

Happy in my own bubble the assassinations, riots, and demonstration my teachers want to debate in class seem distant. Michael connects me to reality with nightly reviews of the latest *Oregonian* headlines: *Cronkite Reports On Visit To Viet Nam; LBJ Withdraws To Seek Unity; Shot Kills Martin Luther King In Memphis; King's Slaying Sets Off Violence In Cities; Demonstrations Protest Viet War; Nation Watches Oregon As Primary Nears.* Although our views on civil rights and the war are similar my family is more conservative. Michael and I agree to disagree about presidential politics. He likes Kennedy. I'm for Nixon since I met him a year ago. Neither one of us is old enough to vote.

Each evening after dinner, I unplug the phone in the dining room and carry it upstairs to the phone jack in the hall between my bedroom and the little room where I study. It isn't easy to distract myself while I wait for Michael's call. Tonight the phone rings later than usual because Michael has an interview with Walter Cronkite at the Benson Hotel. Mr. Cronkite and other TV newsmen are in Portland to cover the May 28th presidential primary the day after tomorrow.

"Hi Mary Louise." Michael sounds breathless.

"How was the interview?"

"What an experience. At first I was so nervous my hands were shaking. I didn't feed the take-up real on the recorder properly. Cronkite stopped the interview when he noticed the tape pooled on the floor then he helped me fix it before we went on."

"It was thoughtful of him to help. Did that make you more nervous?

"No, I settled down when we got back to the questions."

"What did he have to say about the primary on Tuesday?"

"He didn't want to predict the outcome. The only thing he said was if Kennedy wins or even has a strong showing against Eugene McCarthy, the race in California next week will be hot."

"I can't believe you interviewed Walter Cronkite."

"Yeah, he is impressive, but that isn't the most exciting thing that happened tonight. After the Cronkite interview, I waited for the elevator. The doors opened. A man in the back of the elevator nodded. At first I didn't recognize him because I was occupied with my recording equipment. The doors closed. I looked up and there he was…Bobby Kennedy."

"You were alone in the elevator with Bobby Kennedy?"

"Yeah, I asked him how he felt about Oregon. He said, optimistic."

"What was he doing in the elevator by himself?"

"He told me he needed some air. He was going out for a walk."

When I tell Debbie the next day, she doesn't believe me. "Bobby Kennedy in the elevator by himself? That's impossible."

"Yeah, sounds crazy, but Michael swears it happened."

Everything is crazy now. This is my last week of lunches with Debbie. Graduation is on the thirty-first four days away. The noise level in the cafeteria, amplified by end-of-the-school-year energy, accompanies the dance of yearbooks around the room. Debbie passes my *Almanac* back after she writes on the title page of the activities section where she is featured in a photograph, one of the perks of eating lunch with the yearbook editor.

Dear ML – alias "Dear Diary" Our last day as "lunch buddies" is over. It's been great hearing about Michael. I wish you both all the luck in the world. Keep twisting those stems and have a great time in Europe. Thanks for the photo. Forever Friend, Debbie

Is there such a thing as a forever friend? This week we go separate ways each with our own plans for the future. My plan is to deliver my commencement speech on Friday, travel to Europe this summer, study pre-architecture for two years at Portland State College, graduate in three more years from the University of Oregon with a degree in interior architecture then live happily ever after as Mrs. Michael Small.

EUROPE

*W*hen you travel to Europe for ten weeks with nothing more than
a rucksack, you need to pack light.

The reality of that warning is hanging heavy on my back. A gray canvas sack with a flap and string tie at the top filled with thirty pounds of the most essential items in a seventeen-year-old girl's life.

The contents of the rucksack are the least of my worries at the moment. I have no idea what day it is or what time and I haven't been in bed for more than twenty-four hours. The only thing I know for sure is that it is a cool late spring day and I'm standing by myself with a handful of unfamiliar money on Waterloo Bridge over the River Thames waiting for a bus to Beulah Spa in South London. I'm tired, anxious, and homesick.

The journey to this place started yesterday, at least I think it was yesterday, at 4:30 in the morning when my rucksack and I boarded a bus in Portland for a three-hour ride to the Seattle/Tacoma airport. At the airport, I joined thirty-nine teenagers and four adult chaperons on a United Airlines jet for the start of our seventy-two-day American Heritage Association study tour of Europe. Because my first ever experience on a jet airplane ended with losing lunch as we landed in New York, worried chaperons spent the six-hour layover suggesting various remedies for my dizziness and my fear of getting sick on the next flight. Thankfully the overnight Pan American flight to Heathrow Airport ended without further incident.

The first indication of arrival in a foreign country was an accent I heard first on Ed Sullivan four years ago. It was coming from John Lennon, Paul McCartney, George Harrison, and Ringo Starr standing a few feet away from me. I could claim they were waiting for me at the gate, but the truth is they were just waiting. Although a swell of rock star magic rippled through our group, no one else at the airport paid much attention. I thought they looked mangy.

The second indication of arrival in a foreign country was a bus ride on the wrong side of the road. At least is would be wrong in Oregon. Although our bus trip into the heart of London past Buckingham Palace and Trafalgar Square was thrilling, the cars and buses darting in and out of traffic circles made me dizzy again.

Dozens of people and a gray mound of rucksacks filled the room we spilled into from our chartered bus. One of the chaperons stood on a chair so he could be seen and heard above the crowd, "You can leave after you connect with your home stay family. As we announced earlier, you are on your own until tomorrow morning at ten when we meet at the Africa Center near Covent Garden."

Another chaperon read the names of students matching them in twos or threes to names of home stay hosts. One at a time groups of students retrieved their rucksacks and left. Thirty-nine Americans were matched with British hosts while I stood waiting. A chaperon approached, "We just found out that your home stay family was given the wrong information about the date of our arrival. They told us you should take the Crystal Palace bus. Your host, Alan Kingston-Jones, will meet you at the Beulah Spa stop."

This is the reason I stand here alone on a bridge in London with the weight of my rucksack and my fears on my back.

A tall, red, double-decker bus stops in front of me, "Does this bus go to Beulah Spa?"

A young man in a blue uniform looks me over and grins, "Yes that's right duck, we'll get you there."

I mount the steps at the back and show the conductor my handful of money. He picks what he needs and assures me he will remember to announce my stop.

At least forty-five minutes later the bus is almost empty when I step down to the sidewalk across from the Beulah Spa Pub. A tall, husky, balding man with eyes full of good humor and a reassuring smile offers a hearty handshake.

"You must be Mary. I'm Alan Kingston-Jones. My wife Evelyn and our two little girls are eager to meet you. Here, let me take the weight of that rucksack off your shoulders."

The possibility of a trip to Europe never entered my mind before I opened an envelope from the American Heritage Association,

AHA, last August. No one my age has been. A few people I know dream about going. Only rich people go to Europe and my family isn't rich.

I sit on the back step on a warm August afternoon reading about AHA study tours for high school students. On the front page of the colorful brochure, the tours are similar to the one my sister Judy took after high school graduation six years ago. She traveled by train with a group of teenagers to Chicago, New York, Philadelphia, and Washington DC. Every year since then we've received information promoting the same tour. I've already been across country on a road trip with my parents four years ago during the summer Judy spent perfecting a tan at the University of Hawaii. I'm not interested in another long, hot excursion to the East Coast.

On the back page of the brochure a new tour catches my eye: *Study Tour of Europe – ten cities in ten weeks. Home stay in London followed by travel to Paris, Amsterdam, West Berlin, Warsaw, Vienna, Salzburg, Munich, Rome, and Florence. Airfare, Eurail pass, lodging and meals included. Cost $1,100.* Images of places I've seen in movies, magazines, and books float through my imagination.

I take the information into the kitchen to show Mother, "The brochure from the American Heritage Society arrived today. There is a new study tour of Europe on the schedule for next summer. Ten weeks for $1,100."

"Are you ready to sign up?"

"I wish. It's too expensive, but it sounds exciting. There is a home stay in London for the first month and then several cities on the continent including Salzburg. Wow, Salzburg is in the *Sound of Music* my favorite movie. After Salzburg they list Munich, Rome, and Florence. Isn't Florence where Mr. and Mrs. Phillips' daughter lives?"

Yes, Jean and her husband are in Florence. He was the American Consul there. After he retired they decided to stay. They live in a villa. When they were visiting here a year ago last November they had to return to help with flood relief in Florence.

"If I went on this trip, I could see where the *Sound of Music* was made and visit the Phillips' daughter in Florence." I laugh knowing the whole idea is beyond crazy.

"Maybe this is something we should consider."

73

I look at my mother to see if she has lost her mind, "Are you serious? Isn't it too expensive?"

"You have that small trust account from your grandfather. We want to save most of it for college, but if you start out at Portland State and live at home, there might be enough to pay for a trip. Give me some time to think about it. I'll talk to your father."

I'll talk to your father usually means *I'll talk your father out of saying no, always his first response to any idea, and into my way of thinking.* Mother is persuasive. It isn't long before an application and deposit are sent. Confirmation arrives before Christmas.

In January, we attend an information meeting. The room is full of teenagers and parents eager to learn more about the trip. We are given lists of preparations we need to make: passport, visa, physical exam and shots; traveler's checks; books to read; and a night class on Britain to take at Portland State.

Everyone meets again at an orientation session in April, two months before we leave. At that meeting, we are assigned chaperons and we are each given a gray canvas rucksack along with instructions on how and what to pack. Girls are not allowed to wear pants and boys have to leave their blue jeans at home.

Thoughts about showing off Michael, my college boyfriend, at the senior prom and preparation for my commencement speech take over for a couple of weeks in May. After graduation in June, the Gloria La Vonne training comes in handy when I plan my limited travel wardrobe. The rucksack is packed, unpacked, and repacked a dozen times before everything fits. Excitement and anxiety live side by side in my mind and body. Never more than a few days away from home, ten weeks is a long time especially now that Michael is a serious boyfriend.

At 4:30 in the morning on June 18th, I say goodbye to Michael, to my parents, to everything familiar.

London:

I can't believe I'm in London. I write letters to my parents and Michael at a table in a large bedroom above the parlor in my home stay house on Dale Park Road. The window on the other side of the room looks out over a public garden. The smoke stacks of Croydon billow in the distance. Both of my letters end with, "I almost forgot to tell you that I saw the Beatles today. Ringo was standing five feet away from me. They looked mangy."

I couldn't ask for a nicer home stay family. Alan, Evelyn, four-year-old Elizabeth, and Anna, almost two, are making me feel at ease. I helped dry dishes after a delicious dinner. During dinner I discovered that Evelyn spent one year of college in Minnesota where she learned to eat corn on the cob. "We feed it to the pigs here." She told me with a chuckle.

Evelyn stays home with the children and Alan has an office job in insurance. They met at Cambridge. Alan gave me a copy of *London A to Zed,* a travel size book of maps, and showed me how to get to Covent Garden tomorrow morning. Evelyn just brought me a cup of cocoa and a plate of what she called biscuits. They look like shortbread cookies to me.

Number Ten Dale Park Road is my address for the next three and a half weeks. The street is a right turn at the bottom of Beulah Hill. On one side of the road is a row of tall, narrow houses in groups of two. On the other side a fenced garden. In America the houses would be duplexes. Here they call them semi-detached because instead of one attached to another in a continuous row, there is a five-foot space between each pair.

A low fence with a wrought iron gate surrounds a tiny front garden. Steps lead up to the front door on the left next to attached house. To the right of the door is a large window. The attached house is a mirror image. I've never seen gardens this small or houses this narrow.

The yellow door of number ten opens into a narrow hall that runs past a pair of doors to the parlor. The ceiling is at least ten feet tall. Beyond the parlor the hall turns to the right along a long staircase. Opposite the stairs a door leads into a dining room with a fireplace on one side, a playpen in the corner, and a dining table straight ahead. In a small kitchen, visible through an opening in the back wall, a refrigerator the size of a dishwasher sits below the counter and hot water comes from a small tank above the sink. A door to the right of the kitchen leads into a long garden enclosed on all sides by a wall.

My room shares the second floor with a sewing room and the bathroom. In the long skinny bathroom, a small water heater hangs between the sink and a claw foot tub. The toilet tank is mounted high on the wall with a long chain to flush. The room is freezing cold because the window looking out at the wall of another house a few feet away is always open.

My hosts occupy the third floor. A bedroom above mine is for Elizabeth and Anna. Another bedroom over the sewing room and bathroom is where Alan and Evelyn sleep. Every room except the bathroom and kitchen has a fireplace that no longer burns coal. I don't know what they do for heat, but I could use some. Even though summer is two days away, London is still gray and cold.

The next morning I leave number ten at nine-o'clock after a breakfast of Rice Crispies, milk, tea, bacon, toast, and pancakes. There is too much food. If I eat like this every morning, my clothes won't fit.

The first bus from Beulah Spa and a transfer to a second bus at The Strand takes me to Covent Garden just as Alan promised. Now I'm lost in the maze of carts and vendor's stands full of fruit, vege-tables and flowers looking for the Africa Center. The scene reminds me of the movie *My Fair Lady* when Eliza sings *Wouldn't It Be Loverly* in Covent Garden. I ask two women busy with containers of flowers for directions to the Africa Center. They apologize for not knowing the way.

"Luvey, are ya lost?" A burley man who could have stepped out of the *My Fair Lady* movie set touches my arm.

At home I would be suspicious, but Evelyn told me to trust Londoners when they offer help. "I'm looking for the Africa Center. No one seems to know where it is."

"Down that lane a bit luv. The one next to the opera 'ouse." The man points to a narrow street along side a grand building with a temple front. I recognize the opera house from the movie.

"Thank you for your help." He tips his cap and smiles revealing a missing tooth or two. Relieved, I leave the chaos of Covent Garden and find my way to the ten-o'clock meeting with my group at the Africa Center.

I've mastered the subway Londoners call the Tube by my third day in London. We need transportation like this in Portland. It's fast and fun. Inside the foldout *Underground – Diagram of Lines*, each line is mapped out in a different color. Central is red, Metropolitan green, Piccadilly blue. The yellow line, called Circle, makes a loop around London connecting all the lines. Instead of taking the bus all the way to Beulah Spa, I travel from any location north of the river to the Elephant and Castle station south of the river on the brown Bakerloo Line then transfer to the Crystal Palace bus. The bus ride to Alan and Evelyn's is still thirty-five or forty minutes, but from E & C, I can reach any North London destination in a matter of minutes.

Mr. and Mrs. D, chaperons for my group of twenty teenagers, gave us a transit pass on the first day at the African Center. It is my magic carpet to anywhere in London. I show the pass to the ticket taker, push through a turn style then descend a long flight of stairs to reach the trains. A wind greets me from below. The warm, moist air has a smell of earth and humanity. The hum, rattle and swoosh of the trains is now a familiar sound. Crowds rushing to and from Victoria, Westminster, Charring Cross, and Leicester Square draw me into the everyday vibrancy of London. When my train stops I follow the "Way Out" signs to visit a museum, attend a play, or just walk the streets of a city packed with exotic sights, sounds, tastes, and treasures.

We are in Hyde Park watching an outdoor performance of *Merry Wives of Windsor*. It seems ironic to be here on the other side of the Atlantic watching Shakespeare with an English audience on American Independence Day. After the performance we are going to celebrate the holiday with a 4th of July picnic. One student found watermelon and another baked an apple pie. Last night at the live musical, *Man of La Manche*, a Betsy Ross in our group was hand sewing an American flag for the festivities. Everyone feels a little homesick.

Most days there isn't time to be homesick. We are busy with morning lectures at the Africa Center on the education system, government, religion, business, and history. In the afternoon we visit schools, government buildings, churches, and museums. The evenings are filled with theatre performances such as *The Importance of*

Being Ernest, There's a Girl in my Soup, and *Fiddler on the Roof.* One night we went to see *A Man for All Seasons* the new movie about Sir Thomas Moore the man who stood up to Henry the Eighth and lost his head for his effort. We saw the room in the Tower of London where Moore was held prisoner, we visited Henry's palace at Hampton Court, and we saw the famous portrait of the king by Holbein at the National Gallery.

On free day's we can do whatever we like. I went to see the glass and wrought iron Victorian conservatory at Kew Gardens a few days ago. The evenings we have free are spent with our home stay families or writing letters.

Last weekend we visited Windsor Castle. I was fascinated with Queen Mary's Dolls' House. Every detail of the 1/12 scale, three-story miniature house is perfect from the 1920s light fixtures to tapestries and paintings on the walls; tables, chairs, beds, and desks in the rooms; Oriental carpets on the floors. The library shelves hold miniature copies of English classics. This weekend we will go by bus to Canterbury Cathedral.

I'm watching cowboy night with Alan on British TV. He is crazy about American Westerns. Nothing takes him away from the telly on his favorite night of the week. *Wagon Train* just finished. We are waiting for *Bonanza* when I hear the "blurp, blurp" of the phone ringing in the hall.

Evelyn appears at the parlor door, "The phone is for you Mary."

"For me?" Who would be calling me in London?

I pick up the receiver on the table in the hall, "Hello."

"Hello Mary Louise, this is Michael."

My heart flutters at the sound of his voice, my mind worries about why he is calling, "Is everything OK?"

"No, it isn't. I have bad news. My grandmother died last night. She was hit by a car crossing the street to catch the bus after work at Meier and Frank."

I sit down hard on the bottom step across from the phone. Evelyn stands a few feet away, a look of concern on her face. A gunfight on the telly is the only sound.

"Are you still there Mary Louise?"

I find my voice, "This is a shock Michael. I don't know what to say."

"We thought you would want to know. Perhaps you should consider coming home."

All the little bits of homesickness roll into one big lump in my stomach. "How are you Michael? Is your mother OK? I want to be there for you. I don't know if it is possible to come home."

"We are managing. We are good at managing." Michael's family has endured more than their fair share of loss. First his grandfather, then his father, his aunt has cancer, and now his beloved grandmother.

"Your grandmother was always kind to me. We had fun with her at hockey games. I will miss her."

"My three minutes are almost up. I'll write you a letter with the details. Goodbye for now."

"Tell your family they are in my prayers. All my love to you Michael, goodbye."

Evelyn takes the receiver from my hand and replaces it on the phone. She sits down next to me on the step and puts her arm around my shoulders. Tears roll down my face. Sobs shiver through my body. We sit in silence for a long time.

"You have suffered a terrible shock Mary. Take some time to adjust. Don't even consider going home until you let this settle. There is nothing you can do there. The best way to remember her is to enjoy your holiday. She would want that."

Highlights of My Trip:

- London – Home stay family, learning to get around on my own, phone call from Michael about his grandmother's death, fascination with a painting – "A Bar at the Follies Bergere," and the English countryside. Her eyes avoid my glance no matter where I stand.

- Paris – Midnight show at the Lido (champagne), the Mona Lisa, Versailles, ice cream, the city at night

- Amsterdam – van Gogh Museum, red light district

- Berlin – Bombed out buildings, the wall, Russian tanks, haircut

- Warsaw – Radio propaganda, Chopin concert, straw mattress

- Vienna – Pastry, museum overload

- Salzburg – Sound of Music, salt mine

- Munich – Sick on pizza, beer garden, concentration camp

- Rome – Dancing with Italian men, "The Pieta," Apian Way

- Florence – Concert at Pitti Palace, dinner at villa

- Return wearing panty hose and an Italian mini skirt.

COURTSHIP

The Portland Airport vibrates with an uncommon level of activity for two-thirty in the morning. A jumble of voices from eager family and friends reaches me before I glide on a giddy high up the red-carpeted ramp to the waiting room. Not the same girl inside or out who left for Europe seventy-two days ago. I return in short Mia Farrow hair and a Twiggy length mini dress of Italian knit the color of celery. Panty hose replace a girdle. Tampons replace pads. Daddy becomes Dad. I carry souvenirs, a wealth of memories, and a heart happy to be home. Mother, Dad, Judy, Frank, and best of all Michael wave from the crowd clustered behind a railing above the ramp. My traveling companions and I one at a time dissolve into huddled groups of well-wishers generous with hugs and kisses. The lips missed for ten weeks find mine. The arms ached for enfold me in a long anticipated embrace.

An eternity passes before we are home and my parents decide to take a nap. "Don't stay too long Michael, Mary Louise needs to get some sleep after her twenty-four hour journey." Mother gathers me into a hug, "I'm happy you are home sweetie."

"So am I. No more long trips for me." Mother releases her hold on me and closes the living room door.

Michael and I sit side by side on the sofa, "I missed you Mary Louise. After Grandma Kingston died, I needed you even more."

"Oh Michael, I'm sorry you were alone. I thought about you and your family every day."

"We need to make up for lost time." Michael turns off the lamp, slips his arm around, draws me close. In the middle of a kiss his tongue surprises me. While we tongue dual an awkward French kiss Michael's hand rests on the celery ruffles over my right breast. Was his touch an accident?

The few weeks between my homecoming and the beginning of the school year evaporate. We can't get enough of each other. The hand over my breast was no accident.

Less than a month after my arrival home from Europe classes begin at Portland State College. Michael, on the semester system at Lewis & Clark, started two weeks earlier. College exceeds my expectations. Instead of the forced requirements of high school, I choose my schedule: Basic Design, Oil Painting, History of Art, Introduction to Poetry, and Golf as a PE credit. The counselor scares me away from declaring architecture as a major with horror stories about calculus and physics. "Girls who start in our pre-architecture program move into interior architecture when they transfer to the University of Oregon. That way you get the basics of design without worrying about math and science." Any way to avoid math and science sounds like a good strategy to me.

The first month is scary. I don't know my way around and feel like DUMB FRESHMAN is stenciled on my forehead. The classes are harder than high school. Homework is never done. College schedules cut into phone call and date time with Michael. Some weeks I only see him at church on Sunday.

Darey, a friend from backpacking camp two summers ago, replaces Debbie as lunch buddy. After graduation, Debbie disappeared into her own world. So much for forever friends. Darey is a year ahead of me with a major in computer science. Her Dad is an architect. My Dad studies computers. We share an interest in art, hiking, and our backpacking friend Ron, the boy who took me to *Gone with the Wind* last Christmas.

Darey carries stacks of punch cards fastened with rubber bands and folded print-outs wherever she goes. When my dad or Darey try to explain computers to me, my ears glaze over. I don't understand why Darey sits for hours every day in front of a keypunch machine in the college's basement computer room. After the cards are punched she processes them through a card sorter the size of a Volkswagen. The machines spit out nasty error messages when a mistake is made.

"Have you found the error?"

"Not yet. Somewhere in here a mistake has sabotaged the program." Darey unfolds a one-inch thick printout and drapes it across the lunch table.

The Viking Lounge located on the ground floor of Smith Memorial Student Center is a quieter place to eat lunch than the high school cafeteria even though windows look out onto traffic on SW Broadway in Downtown Portland. No prancing or preening cool girls here. Serious students of all ages and backgrounds commute to this urban school. Many sit alone to catch up on studies during breaks between classes. Conversations are quiet.

Round tables in the lunchroom seat six or less if someone like Darey spreads out over the whole table. My design instructor says the trumpet based tables and white molded plastic potato chip chairs on skinny polished chrome legs, were ahead of their time when Herman Miller first produced them in 1950. The design is timeless, but the appearance of the furniture and this lunchroom is past prime.

Pat, a girl I met in Poetry, and Georgina from Basic Design join us. Darey folds up her print out to make room.

Pat settles into a chair opposite, "Still struggling with the error I see." She pulls out a syringe and a grapefruit. Pat uses the grapefruit to practice her shot technique so she can give her father his medication.

Georgina unloads books onto an empty chair, "I can't stay long. My schedule has changed. Today I work one to nine." Georgina supports herself with a job in customer service at Lipmann's Department Store.

Now that everyone has arrived, I'm eager to brag about last night's phone conversation with Michael. "Guess who Michael interviewed for the radio station?"

"Walter Cronkite, Bobby Kennedy's ghost." Darey's error makes her grumpy.

I brush off her comment, "Not even close. He interviewed Jimmy Stewart yesterday. I'm jealous. Stewart is one of my favorite old movie actors."

Pat looks up from her grapefruit, "Wow, how did that happen?"

"One of Stewart's twin daughters enrolled at Lewis & Clark this fall. Michael heard he was on campus for a visit and tracked him down."

Georgina stops in the middle of a bite, "I'm in love with George Bailey in *It's a Wonderful Life*."

"Michael says Stewart is a great guy, easy to talk to, and has a wry sense of humor. He was joking about how much it costs to send his daughter to college."

Darey shakes her head, "Yeah, rich kids attend Lewis & Clark."

The comment touches on a point of contention. Michael's scholarship and survivor benefits give him a free ride to a prestigious private college on a beautiful campus. He doesn't need to work in the summer. Now that Michael's classes have started again, I feel like an afterthought. I tell myself to be grateful. I'm not stumped by an error like Darey, I don't have to pay my own way like Georgina, or have a father dying of cancer like Pat. None of them have boyfriends.

My father's reel-to-reel tape recorder booms an Ed Ames baritone rendition of *My Cup Runneth Over*. Janson's *History of Art* rests on my desk open to a diagram of Doric and Ionic classic architectural orders. Our midterm in Art History tomorrow covers the ancient world including Egyptian, Greek, and Aegean architecture, sculpture, and decorative arts. A few slides are easy to identify because I saw the original on my trip: The Three Goddesses from the east pediment of the Parthenon now in the British Museum, the Dying Gaul in the Capitoline Museum in Rome, and my favorite the Nike of Samothrace or Winged Victory displayed on the landing of the grand stair at the Louvre. My first view of the headless eight-foot winged woman held my feet to the floor, my mouth open in awe.

The ring of the phone in the hall breaks my concentration. That will be Michael.

"Hi Mary Louise, did I interrupt anything?"

"Just memorizing terms of the classical orders sterobate, stylobate, shaft, capital, entablature …."

Michael cuts me off, "OK, I get the idea. Did you read the paper today?"

"The only thing I've read today is Mr. H. W. Janson." I avoid the newspaper for the same reason Michael reads it, politics. I don't need to read the paper. He fills in the gaps.

Michael pushes ahead with his report, "One headline reads, *Nixon Urges Final Push Before Thin Ohio Crowd.* Another, *Humphrey Rally Crowds Sidewalks of New York.*"

"So, your point?" Every few days we argue about the upcoming election. It wears me down.

Michael trumpets, "Humphrey is going to win next Tuesday."

"It scares me to think of Humphrey as president. He would just continue with Johnson's policies. See where that got us. Nixon says he will negotiate peace in Viet Nam." My parents, lifelong Republicans, fostered prejudice in me against Democrats. Mother calls them *Dumb-o-brats.* Dad thinks Michael is a bad influence. When I argue with Dad about Viet Nam he says Michael brainwashed me.

Michael continues to press me, "Doesn't Nixon's *law and order* stance bother you? He is a cagey guy. I don't trust him."

"If you let me have Nixon, I'll let you have Wayne Morse over Bob Packwood for Senate. At least Morse is one of the two senators who voted against the Gulf of Tonkin."

Without conviction Michael says, "That's generous of you."

"Dad won't vote for Morse, but Mother would listen to reason. She opposes all war because she lost Joe in WWII."

"Your Dad would never vote for a Democrat because we are eeevillllll." Michael imitates a Boris Karloff accent.

Although Michael is right, there is no time to talk about our family prejudices now, "If I don't get back to studies, the only evil will be failure to recognize the difference between a freeze and an architrave."

"OK, good luck on your test."

A week later my test comes back with an 'A' and the headlines announce *Nixon Elected President by Narrow Margin, Packwood Increases Slim Vote Lead.* Political discussions end for now.

Light January snow spits against the windows of the lunchroom. The weather forecast predicts another storm tonight like the snow and ice between Christmas and New Year's when Michael injured his left knee while pushing his car up a hill. So far Darey is the only lunch buddy today in an almost empty lunchroom. A few flakes spook Oregonians.

"Did you see *Funny Girl* over the weekend?"

"No, Michael's leg is still in a cast. This knee injury is a bummer. Except for New Year's Eve when Michael's Uncle George drove him over in an ice storm and twice when Gary picked me up, we haven't seen each other. My parents won't let me drive to his house. They say, *it isn't proper for girls to chase boys.*"

"Are you sure this leg thing isn't Michael's excuse to ignore you?"

Intent on finishing my story I ignore Darey's comment, "Picture this on New Year's Eve Michael and I sat in the living room listening to George make small talk with my parents. We couldn't even kiss. Not my idea of a romantic ringing in of the New Year. No homework, no time pressure, and no boyfriend; the whole vacation wasted."

As soon as Darey and Georgina arrive at the lunch table I spill the latest boyfriend news, "Michael sent me roses for Valentine's Day. Twelve long stemmed red roses." I hold back a hint of disappointment about the arrival of the roses in a cheap bubble glass vase instead of a long white box tied with a silk ribbon like in the movies.

"It's about time he started paying more attention to you." Darey's heart holds suspicion of Michael and his motives. She lobbies for our mutual friend Ron.

Darey's criticism gnaws at me. I defend Michael to ease my insecurity, "His knee injury kept him from seeing me."

"Mike attends classes and has time for the radio station, but no time for you. Now that his knee has healed does Gary still pick you up for dates with Mike?"

Gary sits down next to me. "Did I hear my name?"

Darey maintains interrogation mode, "Do you still pick Mary Louise up for dates with Mike?"

"I don't mind. We have fun."

Gary offers me a perfect out, "Yeah, Gary's idea of fun, he teaches me to drive a stick shift on a Mt. Tabor hill."

Gary grins at his opportunity to tease, "You should have seen us buck up the street." He punctuates his statement with an imitation of the staccato movement of the car.

I throw a scowl in his direction, "It wasn't funny when the motor died and the car started to roll back down the hill." A wave of laughter circles the table.

With a mock serious face Gary attempts to redeem himself. "You did well for your first time."

Home from a three-month enlistment in the Army, Gary joined our lunch group in January when he enrolled at Portland Community College next door to Portland State. A doctor, unhappy about his own unwelcome military service, orchestrated a medical discharge for Gary because of his size fifteen feet and painful bunions. A lucky break for an I-A draft number at the top of the lottery list. I'm thankful Michael is IV-A, sole surviving son. He will never be drafted.

I forgave Gary for his part in the *Gone with the Wind* fiasco. His apology seemed genuine. It's impossible to stay angry; he is such a goofy lovable guy. An enthusiastic puppy overflowing with energy and good intentions. How can I resist those deep brown puppy eyes?

Gary must be lonely. Why else would he show up at our lunch table several days a week? He bounces around between his mother's house where his stepfather yells at him, his father's house where his stepmother ignores him and Michael's house. I've known Gary since we were children. He is the older brother I always wished for. Mother would adopt him if she could. Gary times his arrival in Mother's kitchen at dinnertime knowing an invitation will be offered to stay for a casserole and homemade berry pie.

"Hey Gary, tell the girls about your night job picking up dead people for an embalmer."

Georgina looks up from her art history book. "At night? How creepy."

"Yeah, four of us stay all night in a house owned by the medical examiner. He does embalming on the side. When a call comes in, two of us go out with a station wagon to pick up the body and bring it back for embalming. We deliver the bodies to mortuaries after the procedure is finished."

Darey, Georgina, and I are drawn in and repelled at the same time. I can tell Gary gets a thrill from creeping us out with his story.

"On the first night of a new hire, one of us lays out naked on the embalming table in the basement. We ask the new guy to go down and put on a toe tag. The person on the table is still while the tag is wired to his toe then he rises up and shouts, *What the Hell are you doing?* One guy we initiated fled never to be seen again." Another ripple of laughter circles the table.

Gary's stories are better than TV. He is entertaining, but I wonder if he will ever settle down and be serious about life.

Bleachers in the Lewis & Clark gymnasium are packed with students listening to Phil Ochs play the guitar and sing folk protest songs. His music is new to me. I'm surprised by how much I like *There But For Fortune* and *Outside of a Small Circle of Friends*. Michael has introduced me to music, politics, and a view of the world that is outside my comfort zone.

Michael's sister Mary recommended me for a summer job as a cutter in a drapery sweatshop where she has worked for several summers. This summer there are four Mary's on a staff of five. When Millie, the volatile owner of the shop, shouts "MAAREEE" all four of us come running. Two of us are scolded for leaving our work and one for some minor mistake. Michael's sister is never reprimanded even when she forgot to unlock the folder and it tore some expensive sheets. Mary is given preference because she and her mother are in Eastern Star with Millie and her daughter. I live in fear of Millie's wrath. For this torture I make one dollar and seventy cents an hour. Five cents more than minimum wage. Michael has a cushy summer internship at a new food bank.

It has taken months to admit to myself that Darey is right about Michael. He assumes I will be ready to jump whenever he wants me. Several times after his knee healed he told me, "I don't have time to pick you up. If you want to come over, I'll send Gary." As a result, I spend more time with Gary than with Michael.

One July evening the phone rings, "Hello Mary Louise, this is Ron." Ron the friend from backpacking. Ron the boy whose mother drove us to see *Gone with the Wind*. Ron, the scent of English Leather.

"I was wondering if you would be interested in the new Cinerama movie *Krakatoa East of Java* playing at the Hollywood Theater. I've heard the special effects used for the volcano are dramatic on the wide screen." Ron rushes on to say, "How about Saturday? I have my license now."

Watching a volcanic eruption for two hours is not my idea of a pleasant evening, but the opportunity to tell Michael, *Sorry, I'm busy on Saturday night*, is too tempting to resist. "Sure, what time?" After I hang up the phone, I feel evil for taking advantage of Ron.

The movie is loud and the boat scenes on the curved Cinerama screen induce a mild seasickness. In the car after the film, I enjoy Ron's gentle kisses more than I want to. A lost pearl earring goes unnoticed until I close the back door and he is gone. My conscience stops me from accepting another date. Although Ron is a sweet friend, Michael is the one God intended for me.

The strategy worked. Michael is more attentive for the remainder of the summer.

On the last Saturday of August Michael picks me up early. Yesterday I finished my final week of torture in Millie's sweatshop. Today we are going to pick huckleberries with Harvey, the old family friend Michael's grandmother talked about at that long ago dinner.

Harvey's blue van is parked in the Small's driveway when we arrive. A tall lean man in denim work pants and shirt with sleeves rolled to the elbow is loading the back of the van. His hair is gray and thick, his skin weathered by sun and hard work.

"Harvey, I'd like you to meet Mary Louise."

"Happy to meet you." His work worn hand swallows mine in a hearty handshake. "Never picked Huckleberries?" Harvey is a man of few words.

"I've picked raspberries and strawberries for my grandfather."

Harvey looks me over with eyes lit from an inner source, "You'll do fine."

We load into the van. Mary takes the front passenger seat and winds up for a long dissertation to Harvey about her fiancé's naval career. I snuggle next to Michael in the middle seat. Dee Dee sits behind us with her mom. Before we leave the driveway, Dee Dee whines, "I'm hungry. What do we have to eat?" Every few seconds she kicks the back of my seat. This could be a long day.

More than an hour passes. We turn off the highway onto gravel then dirt roads that split into a confusing web through the forest. Harvey knows these roads. He brings us to a clearing where the air is heavy with the scent of fir needles, sun ripened fruit, and the sweet smell of earth. Waist high huckleberry bushes are bent with purple fruit the size of petite peas. Harvey hands each of us a coffee can with a string to place around our necks. The percussive ping, ping, ping as ripe berries drop into our cans is mixed with bird song and the sigh of trees in a soothing breeze. I stay close to Michael; a kiss stolen here and there. Huckleberry picking is my new favorite activity.

Darey, Georgina, and Pat all show up for lunch at the same time on our first day back after Christmas break. Darey starts the conversation, "Tell Pat and Georgina about your wedding marathon."

"I'm on wedding overload; three weddings in ten days. Michael stood up with a friend a few days before Christmas then his sisters were married two days apart during the week after Christmas. Mary and Jim had been planning their wedding for a year. Early in December Linda, the trombone player, announced that she would be arriving from Boston with Ray, ex-marine band trumpeter, to marry two days before her sister. What a mess. Tomboy Linda rented a long white wedding dress and all the men picked up their tuxedos a few days early to wear at both ceremonies."

Pat asks, "Was Mary upset about Linda upstaging her? I would be."

"I would be too, but Mary didn't say anything. What could she do? Linda gets what Linda wants. By the night of Mary's ceremony everyone was tired of weddings."

"Who caught the bouquets? With three chances, you must have caught one."

"I caught Mary's bouquet. She thrust the white carnations in my direction so hard I couldn't miss if I tried."

Pat laughs at the rigged outcome, "I guess this means you are the next bride." I hope she is right.

The day is warm for the middle of March on the Oregon Coast. A steep switchback trail brought us down into a deserted cove seventy feet below the overlook at Ecola Park famous for a classic view of Haystack Rock at distant Cannon Beach. Michael and I lounge on a blanket out of the wind and out of sight behind a driftwood log.

After our picnic lunch, Michael moves closer, slides his hand up under my shirt, unfastens my bra, and caresses my breast. I was shocked the first time this happened. Now I expect his fingers against my skin.

Petting at the end of a date creates so much steam on the windows of Michael's car that the neighbor across the street from my house came out one night to investigate. Since then we moved to the basement party room for privacy. Today there are no neighbors. We are free to explore each other on this beach.

Michael unbuttons his shirt and pulls me up to a straddle position over his legs. His chest presses against my breasts. I feel him hard under me. He unbuttons his Levis and pushes my hand inside to touch him for the first time.

Darey is eager to hear a report about a weekend clamming trip to Long Beach with Michael's family. "Did you find any clams?"

"Digging for clams is exhilarating. As soon as a bubble appears in the sand you have to dig as fast as possible or the clam will bury itself. Even though the beach was crawling with people, we dug our limit in less than an hour."

"How did they taste?"

"That's the problem with clams. They taste awful. Harvey cleaned them then Michael's mom fried them. There was so much smoke coming from the kitchen I couldn't see across the room. The best description I can give of the outcome is tire rubber dipped in slime, breaded with burnt sawdust."

Gary and I stand in the corner of my afternoon design studio at Portland State with a dozen other pre-architecture students. From the second floor windows we have a front row view of the confusion of anti-war demonstrators camped in the Park Blocks. A police presence is visible on the perimeter. Although sympathetic to the anti-war cause after the National Guard shooting of four students at

Kent State, we question the motives of the hippie tent community. Our classes are held hostage by a student strike.

Gary moves away from the window, "We shouldn't waste a beautiful day. Do you want to go for a drive? We can explore the grand old houses in the neighborhood along Vista Avenue or walk through the Rose Garden in Washington Park." The sun and Gary's enthusiasm persuade me.

Gary tosses his books on top of overstuffed paper bags and clothes piled in the trunk of his 1963 white Cadillac, "It looks like you live in your car. How can you find anything in that mess?"

"I have a system." Gary closes the subject with a bang of the trunk, ushers me to the passenger door then slides his six foot seven frame behind the wheel with space to spare.

"You and this tank of a car are in perfect scale with each other. I can hardly see over the hood."

Gary navigates the turns up SW Salmon Street past Victorian and Classical Revival beauties. Several houses are converted to office space. After we cross SW Vista a *For Sale* sign planted in the lawn of a Spanish Colonial home by the entrance to Washington Park invites a closer look.

Gary, always up for an adventure says, "It looks empty. Let's park and peek in the windows."

His boldness overcomes my wariness, "If you find a parking spot big enough for this monster I'm game."

We park inside the entrance to the park and walk back to the pale yellow stucco façade. The front door, under a triple arched porch supported on Doric columns, is flanked by multi-paned French doors. I press my nose against the glass in one set of doors and Gary the other. A rooftop skylight washes the columned entry hall and tiled floor with a warm glow.

"I can picture an elegant Christmas party in this house?" This is one of Gary's favorite fantasies. "I see black tie and elegant gowns around a two story Christmas tree."

Before I have a chance to respond, a figure approaches the other side of my window. The house isn't empty. A woman glares back at me through the glass.

"Gary, we need to get out of here fast." Hearts racing, we run down the porch steps, across the lawn to the sidewalk, and up steps into the park collapsing at the top in a fit of nerves and giggles.

"Yeah Gary, the house is empty. You put us in a pickle." I give him a bad time about his adventures, but there is something about Gary's crazy ideas that pulls me in. I feel alive.

Unfazed Gary tempts me with another plan. "Shall we drive to the beach to watch the sun set?"

"Not today. One expedition with you a day is all I can handle."

The same evening Michael calls from a pay phone in the basement of Smith Center at Portland State. "I can't talk long. The police are moving in on the demonstrators. I sent a feed to the radio station over the telephone." Michael's voice is colored with excitement as though he was on the front line of a battle.

"Be careful Michael. I don't want to bail you out of jail."

Alice drives up and down streets around the University of Oregon campus in Eugene while I scan apartment building *FOR RENT* signs. Credence Clearwater Revival sings *Who'll Stop the Rain* on the car radio. Not a group I would listen to, but entertaining none the less.

I don't know Alice well. She is more Georgina's friend than mine. Georgina can't afford the move to Eugene so Alice is the only other girl transferring from the program at Portland State to the University of Oregon. We are roommates by default.

Alice grew up on a dairy farm in Scappoose, a small community downstream from Portland along the Columbia River. Her mother is Norwegian, her father Polish. Alice's last name, wanting for vowels, defies pronunciation. She has one foot in farm life and one foot on the cutting edge of contemporary culture.

Drawn to the color purple and fascinated with bats after a summer trip to Carlsbad Caverns, Alice refers to herself as the purple bat. Friends call her crazy Al. Her heart is big, her personality bigger. Mother thinks living with her will bring me out of my shell. Life in Eugene won't be dull.

So far the available apartments are out of our price range. My parents agreed to let me live off campus if the cost is at or below the one hundred per month room and board in the dorm. That means fifty per month for my half of the rent and fifty for utilities and food. No wiggle room in Alice's budget either.

We are about to give up when I spot a sign on Alder Street. "Stop! Pull into the driveway so I can investigate." The hand-lettered sign reads *One bedroom apartment, $95/month, ring bell for manager.* We ring the manager for a tour. Not much bigger than a studio a folding screen separates the living room from the bedroom. Windows with a view of fir trees and an old house span the twenty-foot combined width of both rooms. Two blocks from campus, furnished, a secure garage for our bikes, and in our price range. "We'll take it."

During the two-hour drive back to Portland, Alice fills me in on the details of her summer job packing cookies at Nabisco. I share horror stories about my second season in Millie's sweatshop.

The conversation moves to boyfriends, "Michael is driving me to Seattle next weekend?"

"Seattle? Why Seattle?"

"He wants to show me his old neighborhood and take me to the Space Needle for dinner." I secretly hope for a ring in the deal.

SPACE NEEDLE

The elevator to the revolving restaurant at the top of the Space Needle is lifting us five hundred feet above the Seattle Center. That distance insignificant compared to how high my heart lifted a few moments ago when I bumped against Michael's pocket and felt a ring box sized lump. Is tonight the night anticipated since our first date to see *Gone with the Wind* two and a half years ago? Is tonight the night Michael will propose?

Three weeks from now, the first week of September, he leaves for his first year of graduate school at McCormick Theological Seminary in Chicago. He will be gone at least until Christmas, longer if he can't afford to fly home for winter break. Ten weeks apart the summer of my European trip tested me. If he is gone for nine months, I might die of loneliness. I enrolled at Portland State after high school two years ago instead of accepting the full scholarship expected from one of the seven sister colleges on the East Coast, to avoid long separations.

Two weeks after Michael leaves, I move to Eugene to attend the University of Oregon and share an apartment with Alice. The thought of leaving home thrills and terrifies me at the same time.

An engagement is the next obvious step in my relationship with Michael. Last winter when he gave his sisters away and stood up as best man for a friend, a woman at church gave him a good-natured lecture, "I don't want to see you in a tuxedo again until you wear one for your own wedding."

Everyone expects us to marry as soon as Michael finishes seminary. To wait three more years is impossible. Michael will be twenty-three in December and I turn twenty next month. Mother married Joe at nineteen. We are meant for each other. Why wait?

Michael stands close to me facing the windows of the capsule shaped elevator rushing up between the legs of the Needle. His inner child delights in the ride, "The view is great. Look how far we can see."

The elevator lurches. "Maybe I shouldn't look. Elevators and heights make me woozy." I turn to the back of the car. Compared to tourists in summer shorts headed for the observation deck above the restaurant, I'm overdressed in my white sari cloth dress over bell-bottom pants embroidered in gold, turquoise, and salmon. The graceful taffeta lined dress, an out of character gift from my father last Christmas, rustles when I turn away from the view to calm myself. A woman on the other side of the car whispers, "she looks like a bride."

The ride takes less than a minute. The elevator doors open to a paneled lobby carpeted in ruby and gold. When the doors close and we leave the tourists behind, I lean against the walnut wall to settle my head back onto my body. The elevator-ride and the day packed with activities starting with a four-hour drive from Portland this morning has scattered me.

Upon arrival in Seattle, we wandered the aisles of Pike Street Public Market taking in the colors, textures, and scents of seafood, produce, tie-dye, and macramé. This afternoon Michael toured me through his memories in the Green Lake neighborhood where he lived before his father died and his family moved back to Portland. We stay tonight with his family friends in the old neighborhood. It's fun to be on our own here in Seattle. I feel grown up. We can go where we want; do what we want.

Dressed and ready to leave for dinner Michael misplaced his keys. After lifting sofa cushions, checking suitcases, and turning the car upside down for thirty minutes, the keys appeared in the pocket of his Levis. The diversion caused me anxiety about our dinner reservation. Michael, accustomed to losing his keys, appeared unfazed.

"Have you recovered?" Michael steadies my elbow with his hand.

"Much better now that I'm off the elevator."

We approach the headwaiter, "I have a reservation for two at seven-thirty. The name is Small."

The man dressed in black tie checks a book on the stand in front of him, "Yes, I see it here. Come with me sir. I'll show you to your table."

I place my hand through Michael's arm. My fingers tingle against puckered blue and white seersucker stripes of his sports jacket. We are led to a row of tables in front of arched-back chairs wide enough for two then slide across cool vinyl to sit side-by-side behind the narrow table covered in a tangerine cloth. A gold Space Needle decorates the crimson menus placed in our hands, "Your waiter will be with you in a moment. Enjoy your meal."

Seated I take a deep breath. Now I feel solid enough to appreciate the view. Across the aisle in front of us, tables of four or six diners are pushed up against the outside wall. A continuous band of table top to ceiling windows lean out toward a panorama I saw once before eight years ago during Century 21, the Seattle World's Fair. I stood with my family in a slow moving line that summer waiting for a stomach turning ride to the observation deck above the dining room. Back in 1962, the price of dinner in this fancy restaurant exceeded my parent's pocket book.

Green and white ferryboats glide across silky water of Puget Sound. The city surrounds us. It creeps up to the edges of the water in front of us. Canals and fresh water lakes cut through around hills covered in miniature buildings and tiny trees. In the distance, emerald islands dive into salt water below a jagged outline of the Olympic Mountains against a fiery horizon topped by a sapphire sky. Soon the sun will descend behind those mountains leaving us afloat in a sea of diamonds. Tonight a real diamond on my finger is the only precious stone I care about.

"The view is spectacular. I hope we see Mt. Rainier?"

Michael looks up from his menu, "We should when the floor moves us around to the other side."

"After the motion of the elevator, I'm happy this ride is smooth. I don't even notice the floor moving."

"They say the outer ring is so well balanced on ball bearings that a one horse power motor moves the floor, the tables, and the people. It takes almost a full hour to complete the circuit. I made the reservation for seven-thirty to catch the sunset on one turn and the lights the second time around." Michael turns toward me then drapes his arm around my shoulders. "It's like floating on top of the world."

I snuggle closer. A seersucker sleeve against a bare shoulder alerts my senses. My attention circles from the gem-studded vista to speculation about the box in Michael's pocket.

The sun has set. Lights of the city surround us. Ferries twinkle across the broad expanse of Puget Sound backed by the Olympic Mountains against a fading sky. Candles flicker on each table. The waiter clears remnants of Michael's salmon and my plate of half eaten chicken. We order coffee and the Lunar Orbiter Dessert a Space Needle specialty. A few minutes later an ice cream sundae arrives. Cool steam engulfs our table when the waiter tips a pitcher of water over dry ice surrounding the bowl of frozen dessert.

Michael reaches into his pocket, "Mary Louise, I have something to show you." He pulls a small square box out of his pocket and tips open the lid, "Sorry I can't get down on my knee at this table." he holds out the open box, "Mary Louise will you wear this ring? The stones are from my mom's wedding set. It was her idea to use them in a ring for you."

The rolling cloud of steam along with Michael's louder than necessary proposal draws the eye of every diner and waiter within twenty feet. My face is on fire. I take the box in my hand. It holds a diamond encrusted engagement ring intertwined with a wedding ring in a fussy design, each incomplete without the other. Disappointment falls hard on my stomach. This is not my hoped for simple solitaire. I ignore the letdown over Michael's awkward presentation, push aside guilty dissatisfaction with the style, "Oh Michael, it's an honor to wear your mom's stones." I give him a kiss on the cheek.

"I'm sure it's too big, but we can have it sized." Michael slips the ring on my finger; the diamonds fall to the back of my hand. He laughs, "Maybe I should try your thumb or should we keep it in the box until it fits?

Now that I have this ring on my finger no matter what size or design, I'm not taking it off. "I'll wrap this tissue around the back of the band to make it fit."

A lump of rolled up tissue holds the diamonds upright. Michael takes my hand, tips it back and forth, diamonds sparkle in the candlelight, "The jeweler at Stevens and Sons told me the center diamond is a half caret and the total weight is almost a caret. I added some chips to fill in. Mom and my sister Mary helped me decide. This was our favorite."

Michael's enthusiasm softens my disappointment with the design, "The stones are beautiful. I love you Michael."

Michael brushes a kiss across my cheek, "… and I love you. It makes me happy to know you will wear this ring while I'm gone." His smile teases, "When those architecture boys come after you, just wave the ring and tell them you're taken."

"You have nothing to worry about. There is no one for me except you."

I want to get away from the stares of other diners and find a place where we can talk and kiss in private. I want to make plans for our future. I want to know what happens now that we are engaged. "I'm too full to eat dessert. Let's go up to the observation deck to get some fresh air."

"Hold on tight to that engagement ring." Michael snaps the lid closed on the wedding ring and returns the box to his pocket then takes a last sip of coffee and last bite of ice cream.

Michael leaves three twenties on the table with the check. We take a short, smooth elevator ride to the observation deck. Hidden by darkness we kiss then Michael moves behind me, wraps his arms around, we look out at the night from our own world. Like Julie Andrews as Maria and Christopher Plummer as the Captain singing a duet in my favorite movie *The Sound of Music*, "For here you are, standing there, loving me whether or not you should. So somewhere in my youth or childhood, I must have done something good."

A few minutes of euphoria pass before a need to know burns through my hesitation to ask, "Will we marry next summer?"

Michael reaches down to twist my ring between his fingers, "We don't have to decide that now."

Past midnight I lie awake on the lower bunk in a teenage girl's room at the home of Michael's family friends. The Space Needle evening replays in my mind. This is my wished for Jane Austin heroine moment. In the dark I rub my thumb over the ring band stuffed with tissue to prove my memory of Michael's proposal. Now when he goes away to seminary we are committed to each other.

Will my parents let us marry next summer? Will they say I'm too young and should finish college first? Mother will give her support in spite of reservations. Dad will say no, his first answer to everything I ask. He dislikes Michael's liberal politics and progressive religion. Thanks to my conversation last week between services with the head minister at our church, Dr. Russell changed his mind and agreed to let Michael preach before he leaves for seminary. I hope this will show my father that Michael is serious and not a radical.

What will my friends say? Alice told me I should arrive in Eugene uncommitted to take advantage of the twenty boys to one girl ratio in the architecture school. Darey is still suspicious of Michael and jealous of the time I spend with him.

Michael's sister Linda won't be happy. She suspects me of a plot to ensnare her brother against his will. A trombone player and the only woman in a man's world, Linda dislikes me because she sees me as too girly and too conservative. I don't have to be a bra burner to be my own person. I can be liberated without becoming a man.

My mind lapses into wedding planning and bridesmaid dress designs. I picture Darey, Alice, Pat, and Georgina standing at the front of the church in blue, my favorite color, holding armloads of wild flowers. Across the aisle from my fantasy bridesmaids, Michael's love filled eyes connect with mine as I walk down the aisle showered in admiration from family and friends.

One year, I refuse to wait any longer.

EUGENE

Windows backed by the gloomy shadow of fir trees and a dilapidated house mirror the movements of the first night I spend alone in my new apartment. The drapery pulled to the limit leaves me and most of one window exposed. I examine my image reflected in the glass. Although the young woman revealed is eager for independence, I have never stayed alone overnight. The blackness behind the glass grabs onto a lifelong fear of the dark. Beyond the reflection, beyond the blackness, I wonder how to survive the year ahead.

All alone on Saturday night: no Michael, no family, no phone, no radio or TV, and no roommate. Alice works this last weekend, packing Oreo cookies at Nabisco before her parents drive her down here to Eugene on Monday afternoon. Registration at the University of Oregon, two blocks away, starts on Wednesday.

My parents left a half hour ago after they took me out for one last dinner together before they returned to Portland. On the way back we stopped at Safeway to stock my cupboards and refrigerator. Mother gave me a hug and a dose of encouragement, "You and Alice are going to have a great year. I'll come down for a visit in a couple of weeks and bring anything you forgot. Send me a list. Remember, we are only two hours away."

This afternoon Mother helped me clean the apartment and organize the closet sized kitchen. We stacked her old tropical hued Fiesta ware plates in a cupboard, hand-me-down flatware in a drawer, a few well-used pans under the stove. I folded my socks and underwear into two drawers of the bedroom chest. Dresses, blouses, and slacks hang in one of the closets. Art supplies fill half the shelves of a hall cupboard. Toothbrush and toothpaste, eyeliner and shadow roll around my drawer in the bathroom. My only mode of transportation, a purple Schwinn three speed, is locked in the garage under the apartment building. A five by seven photo of Michael in his

101

deep blue suit, white, shirt, and red tie smiles at me from the table next to my pillow. The white walls are bare the "Danish Modern" furniture unfamiliar. Every light turned on in this twenty by twenty foot space won't burn away my fear and loneliness.

Michael left for Chicago on Labor Day almost two weeks ago. He and his friend Tom from Lewis & Clark drove across Canada to Chicago then Tom went on to a Lutheran seminary in Columbus, Ohio. Michael called from a phone booth in Alberta on September tenth, my twentieth birthday, and once when he arrived in Chicago. Three minutes on the phone seemed like three seconds. Every day I re-read the letter that arrived earlier this week. The days crawl along—three hundred and forty three until our August wedding; eighty-six until Michael flies home for Christmas. Maybe when classes start, schoolwork will distract me.

Tonight the only distraction I can think of is to work on Michael's Christmas present, a fisherman knit sweater. The complicated cable design keeps me occupied until my eyelids are heavy. I check the lock and chain on the door, turn off all the lights except one in the bathroom, and hide under my favorite comforter. The bathroom light emits enough of a glow to gauge the security of my surroundings, but not enough to reflect off the glass. Without bright light inside, the fir trees are less gloomy the house behind them less creepy. Stars fill a sky waning to autumn. I kiss Michael's photograph, "Goodnight."

"George, the left ear doesn't match the right." Alice moves my head back and forth, to show Georgina one ear lobe and then the other.

"I see what you mean. This one is too low and maybe not centered." Georgina points to my left ear.

"I appreciate how careful you both are about locating the holes, but if you don't hurry, I may lose my resolve and decide not to let you pierce my ears." Anxiety about a home piercing increases with each minute I stare at a needle, cotton balls, a wine cork, and a bottle of alcohol on the table next to two sterilized gold studs. "Are you sure the ice will numb enough."

"I guarantee you won't feel a thing Zero." Georgina makes another mark on my left ear. "Doesn't that look better Al?"

"Perfect! I guess we're ready for the ice." Alice takes a bowl of ice out of the freezer and places a cube in a damp cloth. "Hold this behind your ear for a few minutes. When it feels numb, you can move it away. George, you need to be ready with the cork and alcohol. I'll do the needle and the studs."

Georgina, we call her George, came down to Eugene yesterday on the train to celebrate her twenty-first birthday. I baked a Bisquick velvet crumb cake. The red candles melted into the hot cake and caught the coconut on fire.

George stayed in Portland this year to work at the phone company. Her parents can't afford to help her with college expenses. Tonight she is a stylish working girl dressed in navy pinstriped slacks and a burgundy turtle-neck sweater with a frosted bob hairstyle, and manicured nails.

Alice, she goes by Al, turned twenty-one a month ago. Al and George are women of the world compared to me. They drink, party, and follow the latest music groups in *Rolling Stone*, the latest fashion in *Vogue*.

Al and George call me Zero because my last name, Ott, sounds like 'aught' another word for the number zero. Al also calls me ML short for Mary Louise. She gives everyone she meets a new name. Bruce, the chemistry graduate student down the hall with a dark mop of hair and nerdy black-rimmed glasses, is called Brucie Willamette after a silly radio show about old Portland and the Willamette River on KEX. Their sister station in Seattle has a similar series with a main character named Percy Puget. Al has renamed so many of our friends that I forget their real names.

Rooming with Alice makes the time without Michael more bearable. The first week she was here we went to see *Wood stock*, a movie about the hippie music festival last summer in upstate New York. The movie stretched my musical experience from familiar Joan Baez to never heard before Janice Joplin.

Mother and Gary drove down at the beginning of October with a carload of essentials I left behind in Portland including a portable record player I've had since grade school. My Straus Waltzes and James Taylor lean against Alice's Credence Clearwater, Jimmy Hendrix, and the tree stump we use as an end table.

Food fills empty spaces between classes and letters from Michael. Mother's homemade cinnamon rolls and cookies offered comfort for a few days after her visit. Alice's family arrived a few weeks ago to celebrate her twenty-first birthday with home canned Royal Anne cherries and fresh milk from her father's cows. Whole, unprocessed milk, a new experience for me. We floated the cherries in sweet white wine topped with whipped cream skimmed off the milk. I might learn to like wine.

All this food means we plan to diet the two weeks before Thanksgiving in preparation for a feast over the holiday. Al's idea of a diet is to follow an all-day fast with a piece of German chocolate cake at the New World Café two blocks from our apartment. A thick piece of moist cake layered with a buttery coconut/pecan glaze and wrapped in chocolate cream frosting equals a whole day of diet calories. We figure if the café owned by flower children serves the cake, it must be health food.

We don't have a lot of free time to fill. Memorizing buildings for *History of Architecture* and designs for a bank project in *Design Studio* along with homework from four other classes keeps us occupied.

The U of O campus is quieter than last spring at Portland State. Tension over anti-war demonstrations on campus has cooled except for a bomb that exploded one Friday night in a restroom on the first floor of a campus building two blocks from here. No one paid much attention.

Letters from Michael arrive every week to ten days full of stories about the antics of young men who attend seminary many of them there to avoid the draft. Phone calls two or three times a month cause more frustration than satisfaction. I hear Michael's voice as clear as though he is in the next room then when the receiver returns to the cradle I miss him more.

The sting of alcohol and sound of Al's voice brings me back to ear piercing, "One ear finished, one to go." She sterilizes the needle while George helps me with more ice.

I reach up to touch the stud in my left ear, "That wasn't so bad except for the sound of the needle popping through my ear."

George assumes a hands on hips stance, "You need to be sure to twist the studs and apply more alcohol at least twice a day."

"Yes sir." I salute and everyone laughs. "What shall we have for dinner? I can't believe I'm saying this, but Al's liver and onions fried with bacon is a winner."

The scent of Thanksgiving morning draws me to Mother's kitchen. Covered with an apron she stands over a pan of onions and celery sizzling in melted butter. The kitchen is as tidy as the cook. Unlike the apartment I share with Al, no dust ball would dare roll on the floor here or dirty dish hide in the oven.

"What can I do to help?"

"Not much to do right now except stuff the turkey and that is a one person job. Just keep me company."

I slide up onto the counter in the corner of the kitchen where children are always welcome to sit. "I brought home this drawing of a wedding dress Alice designed for me." Mother glances up from the turkey to the classic lines of a sleek princess style gown.

"That looks like an easy style to make." Mother, an expert seamstress, sews all her own clothes and most of mine. My sewing skills have improved, but I haven't mastered all the techniques she learned from her mother.

My perch on the counter next to Mother, up to her elbows in Thanksgiving dinner preparation, refreshes our bond enjoyed since childhood. The easy comfort between us emboldens me to bring up a life-long wedding fantasy even though I worry that any mention of Joe might upset Mother, "If I was petit like you, maybe I could wear the wedding dress Grandma made when you married Joe."

Her response surprises me. Not the usual mention of a curse on the dress, "The fit might not be a big issue, but the last time I looked the chiffon sleeves were in poor shape. I don't think they can be saved. The lace panel from the bodice could be re-used in a new dress."

Mother, barely five foot two, has never weighed much more than a hundred pounds. Fifteen pounds heavier and an inch taller I feel like a giant. Wearing her dress never seemed possible. If fit or sad reminders fail to present an issue, I'm determined to make my dream a reality, "May I get it out to see how it looks?"

Mother mixes bread cubes, butter, onion, celery, and giblets together with her hands. The piney scent of poultry seasoning floats across the room. "I need to concentrate on the turkey or we won't have dinner today. Go upstairs and look for the dress in my cedar chest while I finish the bird."

The familiar aroma of cedar fills me when I open the lid of Mother's chest. An arched headpiece made of discolored crepe paper flowers sits in a long tray that moves upward with the lid. Letters from Joe tied with white silk ribbon nestle next to cream-colored satin pumps so small they could fit a child. Aged paper crinkles as I lift out a bundle of tissue wrapped satin, chiffon, and lace. A discolored sleeve slides from under the tissue. I carry the treasure into the kitchen as Mother slides Grandma's familiar dark blue turkey roaster onto an oven rack.

"I found the dress. You were right about the sleeves. May I try it on?"

She wipes wet hands on a towel, "Of course. Let's try it in front of the mirror in my bedroom."

Mother unbuttons a long row of satin buttons. She gathers up the fullness of the ivory skirt and places it over my head. I hold my breath while arms slide into what is left of chiffon sleeves gathered with shirring from shoulder to satin bound wrist. A panel of delicate lace in the V-neckline tickles. Mother comes around behind to see if buttons meet button loops. I'm already in love with the 1939 vintage image I see in the mirror.

"What do you think, can we make it fit? Can the sleeves be replaced?"

Mother's moist eyes glisten in the mirror. "With a bit of adjustment and new sleeves you could wear my dress unless you would rather I make Alice's design."

I turn to give her a hug. "No not Alice's design. This is the dress I will wear when I marry Michael."

Fluorescent lights blind me when I emerge from the darkness of Michael's dorm room at three o'clock in the morning. We fell asleep in his bed. Girls are not allowed on the men's floor after ten o'clock. Earlier in the evening we decided Michael caught on the women's floor would be worse than if I was caught on the men's floor. I pretended to go up to my guest room at ten then crept back into Michael's room.

I tiptoe down the hall to the stair door without making a sound. It groans shut behind me. My heart races as I take the steps two at a time to the women's floor. I reach the door to my guest room undetected. The room dark, the bed sheets cold on my skin, my mind spins too fast to sleep.

I arrived in Chicago three days ago for a spring vacation visit with Michael. This year of separation between Michael in Chicago and me in Eugene is more than I can bear. Michael's two-weeks at home over Christmas just made it harder to say goodbye. Mother understood that we need this spring break together and convinced Dad to pay for my plane ticket to Chicago. She told Dad the trip would give me a chance to see where I will live next year and an opportunity to visit the design school I will attend. Michael assured them we would be under supervision on separate floors of the dorm. Mother trusts me to do the right thing.

I don't mind that things got out of control tonight. We were both aroused by the freedom of being alone. Before long we were naked in the dark under the covers on Michael's narrow bed. His skin was warm, his arms comforting. We were careful to stop before going all the way. I'm not on the pill yet. The feel of damp sheets proved Michael satisfied himself.

Alone in this frigid guest room my body craves the comfort of skin touching skin.

My navy blue Ked's cling to fat nuts attached on each side of Al's front axil. I reach back to grasp any metal I can find to balance weight resting on bicycle handlebars. Al sits behind me in a mini skirt steering and peddling us across campus her left foot shod in a leather shoe the right in a plaster cast. Students stare and point at us. Some flee for safety when Al ding dings her bell.

I can't believe I agreed to sit here. I feel unsafe on a bike in the best of conditions. Last fall I wiped out on wet leaves in an intersection near our apartment building. We were on our way to a seven-thirty in the morning *Plants for Interiors* class, handlebars loaded with dangling milk cartons full of soil. One caught in the front wheel of my bike throwing my cargo and me onto the leafy ground. I came up with leaves smeared across my face like blood. Al expected serious injury under the mess. My pride, injured in front of fellow students, hurt more than the scrapes and bruises.

Nine months ago nothing would put me at risk on the handlebars of a bike peddled by a friend in a cast. A school year of living away from home and rooming with Al opened me. Except for new bellbottoms the outside appearance of the uptight young woman reflected in dark windows nine months ago shows little change. Thanks to Al, I'm a new independent woman on the inside.

Al embraces whatever life offers. She broke her foot sky diving for a PE credit. Last weekend she hitchhiked to Portland for Mother's Day with the cast on her foot. A month ago she stowed away on a train to San Francisco then hitchhiked her way back to Eugene. Her "try anything" attitude is wrapped around a heart of gold. I still wouldn't hitch hike, but I've learned to enjoy a glass of wine.

Today exuberance overcomes fear. Today we celebrate a clear day in May after months of rain and intense studies. Design projects and finals still loom on our horizon, but today the sun shines. Today I celebrate sun and the end of a forced separation from Michael when he returns from Chicago in two days.

Three folding tables set up in the basement party room are piled on top and below with everything from Corning ware casserole dishes and a portable black & white television to leaded crystal goblets and a chest filled with twelve sterling silver place settings. The TV is a wedding present from Michael's mom, the silverware from my parents. Mother has been buying a piece or two at a time since I selected the pattern at Zell Brothers when I was thirteen. My sister and I both have full sets of china, crystal, and silver. Mother never had anything so fine.

A few wedding gifts arrive every day in red, white, and blue US Mail trucks, brown UPS trucks, and green Meier & Frank delivery trucks. Others are delivered in person by neighbors and friends. The in-person messengers enjoy viewing the display in the basement. Some are invited to peak at six sky blue bridesmaid dresses and the repaired wedding dress hanging in Mother's sewing room. The big day is only two weeks away.

Michael comes over every evening to help open the new arrivals and stays late for necking and petting. He looks more handsome than ever with his new longer Sonny Bono hairstyle and moustache. Grandma and Grandpa offered Michael cash if he cuts his hair and shaves his moustache before the wedding. I said, "No way!"

Tonight we are in the basement party room pretending to watch Johnny Carson on television. After my parents went to bed, we began kissing on the sofa then moved to the scratchy rug on the floor in between the tables loaded with wedding presents. I started taking the pill more than a month ago. Now there is no reason to wait until our wedding night.

Michael is on top of me. Neither one of us speaks, we both know where this is going. We fumble our way through an awkward and painful attempt at love-making.

Footsteps on the floor above then the creak of the basement door sends my heart to my throat. I hear the click of the light switch at the top of the stairs then Mother's voice. "How can you see without the light on? It is after midnight, time for Michael to go home."

Caught in the act, we pick up our clothes and rush to hide under the stairs in fear of further investigation. Does she know we are naked? Can she smell our sex?

While I pull on shorts and shirt, I reply with forced dispassion, "The *Tonight Show* just ended. Michael is leaving in a few minutes."

"Don't forget to lock up after he leaves." Mother's footsteps retreat to her bedroom.

The next morning, disappointed with my first attempt at sex, I make an excuse about lunch with Alice then drive to the house she shares with her sister in North Portland thinking she will know how to fix my problem. By the time I arrive, too embarrassed to ask for help, I talk around the subject hoping Al with take the cue. Unsatisfied with more questions than answers, I wonder how to learn about sex.

CHICAGO

Drops of water from a cleaning rag mix with drips of perspiration from my flushed face and cropped hair. I crawl around on hands and knees scrubbing remnants of the last tenant from the tile floor in the apartment I moved into yesterday with Michael, my husband of two weeks. Apartment #703 on the seventh floor of married student housing at McCormick Theological Seminary is our first home. The temperature and humidity in the upper 90s greeted us with a sweaty Chicago welcome when we arrived after a cross-country drive from Oregon. Our 1964 white Rambler station wagon was packed to the roof with dishes and pans, art supplies, winter coats, a collection of record albums, camping gear, and two bikes.

We left Portland the day before Labor Day and camped our way across Idaho, Montana, North Dakota, and Minnesota. A highlight was the Teddy Roosevelt National Park just a few miles east of Beach on the western border of North Dakota. My mother spent eight years of her childhood on that prairie. Desolate country with a rough kind of beauty. The last night we paid twelve fifty for a motel in a small Wisconsin town. Combined with the forty spent on gas and a few dollars for food, the whole trip was under a hundred. On our meager student budget, every penny counts.

Upon arrival yesterday we cleaned the bedroom and made the bed, but I refuse to unpack until every surface is scrubbed clean. The goal is to finish today so I can relax tomorrow on my twenty-first birthday. Every few minutes since early this morning, I empty a bucket of dirty water into the toilet. The transformation from filthy to clean would make my mother proud.

Our new home, consisting of two rooms and a bathroom, is smaller than the apartment I shared with Alice last year in Eugene. The main room functions as living room, dining room, kitchen, and study. An efficiency kitchen fits a gas stove, sink, and below the counter refrigerator into a six foot space at one end. Windows at the other end look out on the tree covered McCormick campus, historic faculty row houses, Lincoln Park neighborhood, and five miles to the southeast the skyscrapers of the Chicago Loop. We can see Lake Michigan due east and Wrigley Field is a ten minute bike ride to the north. Last night the city sparkled like diamonds. This morning muddy smog clouds the skyline.

The seminary constructed this twelve-year-old apartment building in the late fifties using a design similar to the gang infested Cabrini Green public housing project a few miles south of us. As with many low income housing projects in Chicago built by contractors who substituted poor quality materials or disappeared with the money before the job was complete, our bedroom closet lacks doors, the bathroom fixtures have not aged well, and the efficiency kitchen is less than efficient. Ideas for a complete redesign of the apartment float around in my head while I clean my way across the floor.

My drafting and design classes at Harrington Institute of Interior Design begin next Wednesday and Thursday. Michael has a week before his chaplaincy internship at St. Luke's Hospital and two more weeks of vacation before his other classes start. As soon as we get settled, I will look for a job. My parents pay my tuition and help with Michael's. I have to make enough to buy food and pay rent. A question that dirties my thoughts as I clean: how will I find a job in this big scary city? A tape of Mother's advice plays in my head – *one day at a time, one day at a time, one day at a time.*

Michael pushes open the door, his arms full of groceries. Sweat on the tips of long wavy hair calls attention to rugged features. His plaid Bermuda shorts show off tanned muscular legs. My position on the floor accentuates his six foot two height. Good thing I gave him a showy gold wedding ring. Women will know he is taken.

I catch him before he tracks across my work, "Don't walk over by the stove. The floor is still wet. You were gone longer than I expected."

He sets the bags down on an island of dry floor by the door. "I ran into friends who live on the other side of the building. Boy, we are lucky. Dust from the parking lot swirls in through their windows and the noise from the 'El' is so loud we stopped talking each time the train rattled by."

"Did you bribe someone to get the good side?"

Michael laughs, "Mrs. Thompson in student services likes me. How is the cleaning coming along?"

Except for the bathroom the floor is clean. I'm going to let you work on the toilet and the tub. Here, you can empty the bucket and get to work. I'll put the groceries away after I wash out the kitchen cabinet. If I can't reach the top shelf, washing it will be your job. You are a foot taller and have longer arms."

Michael takes the bucket with a frown, "You saved the best for me."

"I don't want to have all the fun."

"Speaking of fun. My friends suggested we go to a German restaurant in the Loop for your birthday dinner tomorrow night. They say Berghoff's wiener schnitzel tastes like Vienna."

"Yum, I remember wiener schnitzel and pastries in Vienna. Is the restaurant expensive?"

"We can use the birthday money from your sister."

I'm wondering what happens when there is no more wedding and birthday money.

The next week I spend Monday and Tuesday on newspaper ads and job applications. The drafting instructor fills the whole eight-thirty to two-thirty Wednesday time slot with a slide show of his projects and tedious drafting exercises. On Thursday, the design of an ad agency in the IBM building is assigned then the instructor dismisses us at noon.

Although I should be practical and use the time for the job search, I decide to walk one block up Michigan Avenue to spend an hour at the Chicago Art Institute. Thursday afternoon is free. I sprint up the grand stair to an Impressionist gallery remembered from my visit to Chicago last spring. A painting larger than any wall in our apartment dominates the room. The life size figures relaxing on the banks of the Seine are familiar George Seurat characters from art history slides. No photo captures the riot of color visible when

I stand with my nose a few inches from small dots of paint dancing across the canvas.

Fueled like an over stimulated child in a toy store, I jump from one painting to another – on the opposite side of the room a van Gogh bedroom; in the next gallery Wood's no nonsense farm couple; around the corner Hopper's lonely souls at the counter of a bright diner on a dark night. No time today to visit the European sculpture gallery or the Thorne miniature rooms. A temptation for another Thursday.

Before I catch the 'El' back to the McCormick campus, I pick up job applications at Carson Pirie Scott and Marshall Field and Company. Both historic department stores advertised in the paper for Christmas help. Shoppers bump into me when I stop in an aisle at Marshall Field to stare at the Tiffany dome above a six-story atrium. Fields could swallow up four copies of the largest department store in Portland.

Chicago beckons me and assaults my senses. Similar to the summer I spent in Europe three years ago, the big city simultaneously revs me up, lets me down, draws me in, and frightens me away.

At the end of September Michael and I celebrate our one-month anniversary with a romantic dinner by candlelight. I prepare stroganoff, bake a cake, and set the table with the two place settings of china, crystal and silver we brought with us from Portland.

Michael takes a bite, "This stroganoff tastes pretty good. Your cooking skills are improving except for pancakes."

"Don't even think about bringing up the burnt pancakes again. I'm tired of hearing about the fiasco on our honeymoon."

Michael chuckles, "Admit it, my pancakes are better than yours."

"OK, I admit it." Then I change the subject. "Did you read the letter from Mother? She invited Gary over to celebrate his birthday before he left for San Diego."

"Yes, I saw that. I can't picture Gary as a police officer, but I guess they are giving him a chance to attend the academy. I could tell the San Diego department a story or two that would scare them."

"And he could tell some on you as well. I think about Gary a lot and hope he finds someone special to take care of him."

"You know he has always had a thing for you."

"No he doesn't. We're just good friends. Gary is more like a brother."

"Who wouldn't fall for those bright eyes and thousand watt smile?"

"I only have eyes for you Michael. Each day with you is better than the day before." While I blow out the candles and lead Michael into the bedroom, I tell myself we are happy here even though Chicago isn't like home. Things don't go well all the time, but at least we have each other.

High above early December Christmas shoppers and giant twinkle lit snowflakes on State Street a tangle of voices competes with shouts from supervisors, "Too many calls waiting. Pick up the pace." On the far wall, visible over the top of row after row of desks similar to study carrels in a library, a few dozen red lights flash a visual image of invisible callers waiting in line for service.

My left ear is numb from a plastic earpiece with attached mouthpiece pressed tight for too many hours by a stiff wire across the top of my head. A cord plugs me into a metal box mounted on the back of my cubicle. Cramped fingers grip a ballpoint pen paused over a completed order form. Stacks of fresh order and return forms fill slots along the back of my desk. Finished forms pile up in an out box on one side. I take in a deep breath of stale over-heated air then flick a switch that connects me to another stranger. One red light on the wall blinks off.

"Marshall Field customer service, may I help you?"

A woman's voice replies, "I need to schedule a pick-up."

"Marshall Field is happy to pick up your item. Please give me your name, address, and account number."

"I'll give you my name. You have the other information in your file."

"I'm sorry, but that information is not here in front of me. We wouldn't want to make a mistake and go to the wrong house." I roll my eyes and mutter in my head about the self-absorbed attitude that dominates this city,

"If you insist."

The woman gives me a suburban address at least an hour from downtown. Then I come to the last question on the form, "What is the item you wish to return?"

"Tweezers."

"Tweezers? Are they defective?"

"No, I just don't need them."

I want to laugh or make a rude comment, but decide not to. I wonder if it isn't a stretch of Marshall Field's famous "the customer is always right" policy to travel that far for tweezers.

"The earliest the driver can pick up your item is Thursday afternoon. Will you be home?"

"No, I'll leave the tweezers in the garage."

"Tweezers are small. How will the driver know where to find the package?"

"Oh, he comes here every week or so. He won't have any trouble. I'm in a hurry. Are you done?"

"Yes, thank you for calling Marshall Field customer service." I flip the switch to cut the connection before frustration spills out of my mouth.

This three day a week job for two dollars and ten cents an hour was an interesting challenge until I learned how to fill out all the forms and answer all the questions. Exploring this beautiful old department store was a treat for the first month. Now the job and the fur draped shoppers on every floor are reminders of what I dislike about Chicago: money powered narcissism and a wide gulf between those who have and those who have not. A guilt pang twitches. I shouldn't complain. At least the ninety dollars earned every two weeks pays for our food and rent.

Settling into our first apartment together and exploring Chicago was exciting until our schedules overflowed with school and work. We don't have much time together. Michael stays up until after midnight every night to watch Johnny Carson and slog through Hebrew. All I do at home is clean, cook, wash, study, and help Michael with his papers. No energy for sewing with the machine Mother sent for my birthday. No time for visits to the museum.

No one here fills the hole left by absent family and friends. Thanksgiving was a disaster. We hovered on the fringes of the community gathering in the commons unconnected to any group. After dinner when we walked the streets of our Lincoln Park neighborhood, a depressing glow of holiday celebrations poured out of house after house. Michael decided we should go home for Christmas. His mom will pay for his ticket and my parents will pay for mine. I already dread our return after the holidays.

When I arrive home from work Michael sips from a favorite coffee cup his Hebrew scattered across the table, "Any crazy customer service stories today?"

I feel too pinched to tell him about the tweezer lady. "I've reached the limit with my job and Chicago. We need to talk."

"Can you wait until tomorrow? I have a Hebrew assignment due in the morning."

A raw crack in the dam held together for months with the glue of positive thinking breaks open. I sit down hard on a chair. Tears and a torrent of 'poor me' complaints flood the room.

"I ride a merry go round to nowhere talking to spoiled rich people for hours on the telephone. At least you're doing something worthwhile when you work with the poor at Cook County Hospital. School is no better. In drafting, we draw construction details for banks and law offices as though the perfect installation of a piece of rosewood matters. The latest design assignment is the interior of a party plane owned by a rich guy who entertains on flights between Chicago and LA. No one at my school understands me. When I showed Phyllis and Jack the *Oregon* book, they said no place could look that beautiful without special camera filters. Does a camera filter create a mountain or a waterfall? No!"

I pause to wipe my nose. Michael is quiet. "When I get home you're busy with your studies or out with friends. I have no friends. I pay the bills, I cook, I clean, and I wash to make life easier for you."

Michael looks at me to see if the flood is spent then launches into a script introduced during our last argument. "You do everything and I do nothing. Your life is hard and mine is easy. Everything is black and white for you. Who do you think made plane reservations for the holidays?"

I try a different approach, "I'm happy we are going home for Christmas, but we will return to the same problems in January. You have another year of seminary after this. How long do I have to wait to finish my degree at the University of Oregon?"

"Of course, I want you to finish your education." Michael stops to see if his statement registers. "My advisor told me about an internship at the Oregon State campus ministry in Corvallis. He says it would look good on my resume. If I get the job in Corvallis next year, you can commute to Eugene to finish your fifth year. Corvallis is only fifty miles from Eugene.

"Oh Michael, do you think there is any chance you can work this out? I could tread water through this year if we go home to Oregon at the end."

I cry my way back from Portland to Chicago after Christmas. Michael sends a letter and resume to the Presbyterian campus minister in Corvallis. I tread water.

In January, Marshall Field cuts me to two days a week, I complete the first semester of classes at Harrington, and Michael passes Hebrew. On the coldest day of the year, I bundle into layers of wool to experience minus fifteen-degree air. Daggers of cold stab my throat. No wonder the patients Michael sees at Cook County Hospital lose fingers and toes to frostbite. Mine are frozen as soon as I exit the apartment building.

February brings a new semester, a job search, and a smelly thaw. By the end of March, I quit Fields and start a new job as the weekend clerk in a laboratory at Children's Hospital two blocks from the McCormick campus. Better pay, fewer hours, and heart wrenching satisfaction from a job involving the care of sick children.

An acceptance letter for the campus ministry internship arrives from Corvallis in April. We call home with the good news. I mail my application for re-admittance to the University of Oregon.

May begins with an obnoxious 'bombing for peace' speech by President Richard Nixon. The next day I send my parents a five-page manifesto on my views about the war in Viet Nam. No reply.

I help Michael photograph mausoleums in a ritzy cemetery for a slide show on the symbolism of death set to Blood Sweat and Tears version of *And When I Die*. The project consumes him and distracts from other classes forcing an incomplete in Old Testament.

After my classes end in June, weekdays are uncluttered. I pay bills, cook, clean, wash, and still have time to sew shorts, halter-tops, a bikini, and a Muumuu. Michael and I have more time to spend together. We ride our bikes to the lake and walk to a Cubs game. My parents visit. No one mentions the war or politics.

Also in June, Michael begins driving swing shift bus routes for the Chicago Transit Authority. The down side of the job with CTA means his Sony Bono hair and sideburns go, the trimmed moustache stays. The up side – twenty-five hundred dollars earned over the summer, a trade in on the Rambler, and a thousand dollar loan from Michael's mom will pay for a 1972 Volvo station we order at the end of the month. Michael wants me to drive a safe car when I travel a hundred miles a day between Corvallis and Eugene to finish my degree.

The Republicans nominate Nixon to run for a second term at their July convention. We mount a McGovern sticker on the back window of our new Volvo the day we pick it up from the dealer. To break in the car we drive in air-conditioned comfort to visit Michael's sister Linda and her husband Ray in Detroit. Ray's gracious hospitality softens Linda's hard edges.

In August at the Democratic convention in Miami, liberal delegates outmaneuver Chicago's once powerful mayor, Richard Daley. I watch the prime time drama on TV. McGovern wins the nomination. Michael gives notice at the CTA. I give notice at the hospital. Gauss, the weekend lab manager from Pakistan who cheers me with his singsong storytelling and genuine kindness, appears sad to see me go.

Its a few minutes before midnight on Labor Day. I wake up from a fitful nap on a bare mattress. The apartment, empty except for the motel modern furniture we found when we arrived a year ago, lacks personality. Everything we own is packed tight in a forest green Volvo station wagon parked in the dusty lot on the other side of the building. The clean rooms, tastefully painted cream with chocolate and chartreuse accents, look nothing like they did the day we arrived. Although I close the door on apartment #703 for the last time, it continues to haunt me.

Behind the wheel in the quiet of the night, I remind myself not to be afraid of the clutch. At the turn of the key, life giving classical music fills hot and muggy end of summer air. The next stop is the Chicago Transit Authority bus barn. After that, Oregon.

CORVALLIS

A shrill train whistle pierces the night. I look up. A steam engine with a cowcatcher roars at top speed toward me. My body lies in the train's path immobilized by terror, no possibility for escape. The engine reaches the end of the bed I share with my husband. It rips the mattress down the middle between us throwing bed-covers over me. Heavy blankets weigh me down; trap me without air to breathe.

The screech of metal against metal wakes me to the rumble of a train on tracks a half block from my apartment. I gasp for air. My heart pounds in my ears. Sweat soaks my nightgown. Will I ever acclimate to this middle of the night assault on sleep? I see the shape of my husband next to me. He appears deaf to the noise. He sleeps through every night unaffected by the train or my nightmares.

I lift my head to see the time. Hands on the lighted dial of our clock radio point to four-fifteen. Although wide-awake, I'm not ready to get out of bed into the cold.

Michael and I moved into our apartment two months ago when we returned to Oregon from Chicago. His internship at the campus ministry across the street from Oregon State University brought us here. Even though the opportunity to live closer to home and finish my Interior Architecture degree at the University of Oregon in Eugene was full of promise, life here is difficult.

Upon arrival in Corvallis we discovered another couple occupied the spacious apartment we were promised on the second floor of the charming English Tudor campus ministry building. Michael's supervisor offered us two rooms in a communal house across the street. I refused to live in the smelly old building with rotting floors and vines snaking through cracks in the walls. A hundred mile a day commute to finish my degree in Eugene is stressful enough without the chaos of a commune. At least this cheap apartment by the rail-road tracks gives us privacy.

Like a robot, I drive the same road to Eugene every weekday morning and every evening. At first the tapestry of rolling farmland and an occasional small town held my interest. Now, deep into autumn, a curtain of darkness blocks the view of everything except a few hundred feet of empty road caught in the headlights.

I looked forward to reunion with Alice, my former roomy, but she has a new roommate and new friends. She complains about my attitude, "You've changed. Chicago made you cynical." No one understands the relentless battering that comes with living in a big city like Chicago. I had to wrap myself in a protective coat of atti-tude to survive.

Last weekend when we visited family in Portland for Thanksgiving, I argued again with my father about politics. He refused to ride in our car unless we removed the McGovern sticker on the back window and expected me to ride in his car with a Nixon sticker. Grief over the outcome of the election is too fresh. The only solace – McGovern won Oregon.

The sound of Michael's quiet breath next to me in the darkness fills me with love for him and sadness. I feel excluded from his life. He hangs out all day into evening at the campus ministry drinking coffee and shooting the breeze with students. If we lived upstairs as promised, I could be part of the community. My schedule pushes me to the fringe.

I look at the clock again, quarter to five. I might as well get an early start on the day. Maybe I just need fewer nightmares and more sleep. After the term ends in two weeks I will enjoy the vacation at least until my wisdom teeth are pulled two days after Christmas.

Summer shines through tiny windows high on the wall in the basement party room at my parent's home. Furniture is piled in the corners of the room to make space for a Ping-Pong table covered with drawings and materials for my thesis project, the redesign of the married student apartment building where we lived in Chicago. No summer for me. I have two incompletes from spring term to finish by the end of August so I can graduate.

I spent three weeks in July building a settee and stools to satisfy the incomplete in Furniture Design and Construction. We drive to Eugene next week for a review with the faculty. I have to finish all the projects before we move to Spokane in September. Michael decided to take another year off from seminary. He enrolled in a counseling program at Whitworth.

I hear Michael's footsteps on the stairs. He stands at one end of the Ping-Pong table. I lean over a floor plan at the other. We take these familiar positions to lob insults at each other across the table.

"It's too hot to paint today. I'm meeting Joel at ten for a hike."

"Every day you say it's too hot. You agreed to paint the house in exchange for living here. At this rate you won't finish before we leave for Spokane."

"Just because you don't want to have any fun this summer doesn't mean I can't.

"I'd like to have fun, but I have to finish my projects. Unlike some people, I finish what I start."

"At least the program in Spokane means you won't have to go back to Chicago next year."

Michael is right. I'll do anything to avoid return to Chicago.

A week later I set up my sofa and stools in the cavernous design studio of the interior architecture department at the U of O. Relief washes over me while I watch Professor Johnson, head of interiors, shoot photos of the completed project. Professor Hawn approaches from across the room. A few feet away his fat face twists into a devilish grin, "Let's see if your piece of furniture passes my test." He sprints the final distance then does a cannon ball into the middle of my settee. A snap like the sound of a starting gun echoes off concrete walls in the empty room. The tearing of wood fibers cracks me open inside. Anger ignites, looks for a place to escape, a place to burn. I suffocate the flame.

SPOKANE

As if cracking the leg on my settee isn't enough, I drive seven hours from Spokane to Eugene at the end of September for my thesis project design review. When I arrive, Hawn and Johnson are surprised to see me even though I verified the date and time by letter. They give a year's worth of work a cursory once over and pass me for graduation. I won't be cheering for the Ducks any time soon.

After we move to Spokane, a different reoccurring dream replaces the train nightmare. In each dream I walk near water on a beach or a dock or a street lined on one side with buildings. Instead of the shriek of a train whistle, there is no sound. Like an ocean, the water pulls back creating a wave taller than a ten-story building. It falls over me. I surrender without a struggle.

No reason for nightmares. I love Spokane and our spacious apartment in a historic building a few blocks up the South Hill from downtown. The manager told us the mayor lived in this third floor unit when the building was built in 1908. Our Chicago apartment would fit into the living room and entry hall. There is ample room for the few pieces of furniture we brought from Portland. My repaired settee sits on the hardwood floor in front of a green tiled fireplace with a dark mahogany mantle. Most residents are twice our age. I take homemade cookies to the lady below us to make up for the noise of our feet on the floor over her head. A woman upstairs invited me for tea. The elderly residents enjoy having us here. They think we are a cute couple.

This charming old city on the eastern border of Washington State is split into North and South by the I-90 freeway. The road travels west through golden wheat country, to apple orchards in the middle of the state, and then after a descent from snowy Cascade mountain passes into Seattle. Going east the freeway winds along Lake Coeur d'Alene in Idaho and climbs into the Montana Rockies.

Spokane, the largest metropolis between Seattle and Minneapolis, has a bit of a wild-west feel in character and setting.

Hot and dry summers here are followed by cold and snowy winters. I delight in snow. Michael and I go for walks in the snow down by the river. It runs through a new park under construction for Expo '74, the Spokane World's Fair. Temperatures in the teens transform the rocky river gorge into a frozen wonderland.

Thanks to OPEC's oil embargo the economy is a mess and there are no jobs for recent graduates. Lines at gas pumps wind around the block even with odd and even day rationing. Last month outdoor Christmas lights were banned as an energy conservation measure. Letters to more than forty architecture offices produce a few fruit-less interviews. I compete with legions of experienced applicants laid off by the recession. Professors Johnson and Hawn help star students like Alice find positions in Portland at big firms. Up here in Spokane, I'm on my own.

The Crescent Department Store, owned by Marshal Fields in Chicago, hired me for their Christmas shop. Now that the holidays are over, my hours are down to two days a week and I rotate around the store. I applied for jobs at the world's fair, but that doesn't open until May.

Michael's days are filled with studies and group meetings. He spends evenings watching television, going out with friends, or attending youth activities at St. Paul's Methodist church where he works a few hours a week. We have an ongoing disagreement about how little time we spend together.

"Do you have a youth group meeting tonight?"

"No, it was canceled."

"Does that mean we have an evening free? It's supposed to snow again tonight. Maybe we could go for a walk down by the river."

"I can't. Joyce wants to get together to plan the communications workshop."

"I thought you already met with her last week."

"That was a brainstorming session. Now we need to work out the details. I told you I wouldn't be home evenings this week."

"You always have something better to do than spend time with me."

"Here we go again. You are either nagging me about irresponsi-bility or complaining because you don't get enough attention. This passive aggressive 'poor me' thing is irritating."

"I'm not passive aggressive. I'm stating a fact. You have plenty of time for your touchy feely friends."

"At least my friends are in touch with their feelings and don't try to lay guilt on me. You have some issues from your childhood to work out."

"Issues from my childhood? I'm your wife not one of your therapy clients. Stop practicing psychoanalysis on me. I'm not a guinea pig."

Michael stares at me for a moment. Without a word he grabs the red and black plaid jacket I sewed for his Christmas present and escapes from the apartment.

Not long after the door slams, my anger begins to mix with regret. Tears sting my eyes. I go to the window. Michael's footsteps in the snow leave a trail across the courtyard. Why do I always bring up issues that cause arguments? I collapse on the settee and surrender to regret.

A ring of the doorbell startles. It sends me to the bathroom to dry tears and check the mirror for signs of my meltdown. Another ring sounds before I reach the door. Please let it not be a neighbor who heard the argument.

I inch the door open. Gary wearing a stocking hat and snow dusted jacket smiles down at me from the dark hallway.

"Gary, I didn't expect you tonight. Michael's gone out. Come in." I turn and walk into the living room to hide red eyes. He closes the door and follows me.

Gary moved to Spokane a few weeks ago to attend the police academy hoping for a job with the police department. He aban-doned Portland to forget a girlfriend who broke his heart.

"I came by to see if you want to go for a walk in the snow."

I look out the window. Fat flakes swirl past. Footprints in the courtyard below are covered with a layer of new white fluff.

He bends over to look me in the eye. Are you OK? Is some-thing wrong?

"Nothing really, just a silly disagreement with Michael."

"Do you want to talk about it? I owe you after the time you've spent listening to me talk about Kathy."

I divert the conversation back to Gary, "Are you feeling better tonight? You were pretty broken up the last time I saw you."

"There's nothing I can do about it now. Kathy wants someone who will marry her and take care of her kids. I'm not ready for kids. I thought we could work it out, but she didn't want to wait."

"I'm sorry Gary. You deserve better."

"That's enough about me. Let's go for a walk and enjoy this beautiful snowy night."

On a dark May evening four months later, my late shift at the Expo '74 Kodak Pavilion over, I walk home through deserted downtown streets. The creepiest part of the route is under the railroad tracks and the I-90 freeway. There are sufficient shadowy hiding places for my mind to conjure up dangerous characters. Most nights I feel safer after emerging from under the freeway, but tonight there are no cars on the street.

Three blocks from home faint footsteps sound on the sidewalk behind me. I look over my shoulder, catch a glimpse of a man a half block away then pick up my pace. His footsteps quicken. Taxed by the incline my heart races. The man rushes up against my back. I feel his hot breath on my neck. He shoves his hand under my skirt, between my legs, into my underwear all the while forcing me down to the sidewalk. His spits a hoarse whisper in my ear, "You want it bitch."

Frozen by fear, I can't cry out, can't think. I feel the umbrella under my right arm. A force comes to life inside my body. My arm jerks back with unexpected strength. It jabs the pointed tip of the umbrella into the center of the attacker's body. The man screams a high pitched, "Bitch!" He drops his hold on me, staggers across the street out of sight.

I'm left in a heap on the sidewalk shaking. Violated, dirty I gather myself.

Without knowing how, I find myself in the entry to our apartment. Michael's nightly television drones in the living room. Purse, umbrella, coat drop to the floor. I bolt to the bathroom, pull off torn panties, wash myself, and wash myself again. No amount of washing will remove the feel of his fingers inside me. Shaking, sobbing without tears in front of the mirror, I brush aside a disarray of hair fallen out of pins that bound it in a tight bun. A face of shame stares back.

Michael opens the bathroom door. "What happened to you?"

Still shaking, I relay my story. "Should I report this to the police?"

"I can understand why you would be upset, but are you making too much of this?" Michael strokes the stubble of his new beard as though reflecting on the validity of my account. "Maybe he wanted to steal your purse. No point in filing a police report. There isn't anything they can do. Nothing happened."

Is that true? Nothing happened? Am I too embarrassed to go to the police? What would I say? A man put his hand up my skirt, end of story.

The next day Gary stops by while Michael is at class. The attack still fresh, weighs on me. I need a strong ear. "A man attacked me on the way home from work last night. He knocked me down."

Gary places his hands on my shoulders his soft brown eyes fixed on mine, "How awful. I'm here to listen." His forehead wrinkles, "I hope you reported this to the police."

"No, I don't know what to report. Michael says I overreacted. Maybe he's right."

At the end of my next late night shift, Gary stands like a sentry across the street from the entrance to the fairgrounds waiting for me. He straightens himself up to every inch of his six foot seven and smiles down at my five foot three. "Do you want company on the walk home?"

TRIANGLE—OPEN MARRIAGE

Michael's knees press against my back in our zipped together down filled sleeping bags. A regular rhythm of his warm breath on my neck proves he is asleep. The fake lemon scent of insect repellent mixed with sweat and smoke from embers of a dying campfire upset the freeze-dried dinner in my stomach. Space is tight in this four-person tent I sewed from a *Frostline Kit*. I'm sandwiched next to my husband between the feet of our two tent mates. My divorced friend Jonnie asleep on Michael's side, and Gary restless on mine. Today we hiked up to a campsite on a cloud-covered ridge in the North Cascades wilderness with a group of friends.

I reposition myself to find a more comfortable spot on rocky ground un-cushioned by a thin blue foam mat. Physical discomfort isn't the only reason I can't sleep. I'm lying between my husband and the man he suggested to me for an affair.

Michael with his tall muscular build, collar length hair, and bushy dark beard sees himself as the virile mountaineer. I watched him ahead of me on the trail this morning dressed in hiking shorts and a tight shirt. I find the curve of his fit body appealing even though his interest in me has waned. A few days before we left for this end of summer backpacking trip he told me I'm not as exciting to him as the high school and college girls he met while a counselor at church camp. "They smoke pot and swim naked in the lake." He tells me. "The problem with our marriage is that you're frigid. You would be more interesting if you had an affair. How about Gary? He has a thing for you."

Nothing Michael says surprises anymore. Truth is he wants sex every time I touch him and in five years of marriage no liaison has lasted more than a few seconds. I thought it was all me until I read *The Sensuous Woman* this summer. Now I know what to expect and in spite of his physique I'm not sure he can deliver. I also believe there is more to a loving relationship than sex.

I feel Gary roll against my leg then pull away. Neither one of us finds a comfortable position. We are silent prisoners in this tent until daylight.

This afternoon Gary steadied me on stones across an ice-cold stream and carried my pack to the other side. Our friendship goes way back to childhood. Unlike Michael, he cares about me as a person not what I do to stroke his ego. Gary -a taller leaner version of Michael's six-foot-two build -is less mountain man, more dashing police officer.

Gary is an honorary member of my family, a brother. Typical of a brother he didn't listen when I warned him a year ago not to marry a woman he didn't love. The night before the wedding he almost backed out, but decided he couldn't let her down. Now they live together in separate rooms. We invited him on this hike to cheer him up.

I hear Gary turn again. We are both miserable. What if I take Michael up on his suggestion of an affair?

How did I fall from happily ever after with the husband of my dreams to an affair with Gary Howarth? The affair was Michael's idea. The stage for it was set last summer when he came home from a week as a counselor at Camp Indianola. "Why can't you be more laid back like Kathy and Sarah? We had so much fun skinny dipping in the evening under the stars."

"Is that when you almost lost your wedding ring in the sand?"

"I always take it off when I swim. It was dark when we came back to the beach."

"Do you think it was wise for the youth minister to go out at night with the teenage girls you were supposed to chaperon?"

"See, that's what I mean. You're too uptight."

"Someone has to be responsible. I spent the week vacuuming the halls, mopping the laundry rooms, and cleaning the pool to keep Mrs. Wormtongue upstairs happy so we can continue to live here in this apartment without paying rent."

Michael replies, "I knew we would get around to you do everything and I do nothing." I decide not to respond. Nothing will change if I do. Michael is quiet for a moment as though he is uncomfortable about what he wants to say next, "Diane was at camp. We spent a lot of time talking about how people are changing their view of relationships. She and her husband have an open marriage. Monogamy is over rated and out of date. Open marriage is the wave of the future."

Not this open marriage conversation again, I think to myself.

Michael continues, "I've decided that I want to stay married, but I need more freedom to be with other women. You would be more interesting if you had an affair. Gary's always had a thing for you. He would be safe."

This conversation should raise red flags for an intelligent and rational person. Instead I say to myself, why not, I'm a modem woman. To Michael it is all about sex. To me it is more about companionship. Falling in love isn't part of the plan.

Two months later in September, I'm visiting with my family in Portland to celebrate my 26th birthday. As usual Gary is a dinner guests. After dinner he says, "It's a beautiful evening, would you like to walk up to Mt. Tabor Park and watch the sunset?" "Sure, I haven't done that for ages. The walk will give me a chance to try out my new Senorita Cortez Nikes."

My feet and heart feel light as I skip down the driveway next to Gary.

"Don't keep MaryLouise out too late Gary. She has a train to catch in the morning." Mother waves to us as we round the comer.

I remember little about the sunset, the walk, the park, or how we managed to spend four hours doing nothing. I do remember how the night ended.

We've been gone for hours. We talked, laughed about high school escapades, meandered around the park, played on the swings and slide, took the long way home. Somewhere along the way our hands found each other.

A block from my parent's home Gary stops, turns me to face him, reaches down to cup my face in the long, gentle fingers of both hands, bends his six foot seven height to touch my lips with a tender kiss that sends a rush of unexpected feeling through my body.

"I love you MaryLouise. I've always loved you." I don't expect anything from you in return, but I want you to know you are loved."

Two months later, the first week in November, I'm on an Amtrak train bound for Portland. Michael took me to the station in Edmonds. He knows where I am going and why. Did I want him to say, please don't go? I love you and want you to forget about Gary? Would it have made a difference?

I look out the window with my reflection in the foreground and Puget Sound backed up by the Olympic Mountains in the distance. I see myself in the glass and wonder, who is this woman? Did she agree to spend a weekend with Gary at the Oregon Coast?

Gary has been in my life since I was five. Every Saturday morning he lounged with a book in the big chair at one end of my Living room while I sat on the piano bench next to his father, my piano teacher, at the other end of the room. We attended the same preschool.

In junior high, high school, and college we hung out in a youth group together and became friends. His six foot seven height next to my five foot three, made us quite the Mutt and Jeff duo. When we attended Portland State College, Gary often showed up at the door to my afternoon studio classes with a plan to drive around the West Hills looking at old houses or sneak off to the beach to watch a sunset. Gary liked to tease. He taught me to drive a stick shift on a Mt. Tabor hill.

When I was a freshman in high school I decided to marry Gary's best friend Michael. Three years older, tall, and handsome and on his way to a career as a minister, he seemed like the perfect catch. I imagined he looked a lot like Joe and as a preacher's wife I could follow in my grandmother's footsteps. It took three years of flirting to snag a first date to see *Gone with the Wind.* Gary almost nixed the deal by telling Michael about my date with another boy to the same movie the night before.

After he turned eighteen, Gary lived with Michael's family. Sometimes he chauffeured me in his 1963 white Cadillac to dinner at Michael's home. He was an usher at our wedding. There is a photo of him throwing two handfuls of rice in my face. When he married, Michael was his best man and I poured coffee at the reception.

Gary spent so much time at my house that Mother expected him to be around for dinner even after I left home. He loved to help eat her pies and spend time with my extended family.

The train jerks me out of my thoughts. We are stopped to let off passengers in Chehalis. Next stop Vancouver then Portland. The closer the train moves toward the destination more nervous I am about the decision made by the woman reflected in the glass. My stomach flutters with anticipation and anxiety. When the train is up to speed again, I see miles of houses and farms, trees, rivers, and roads blur by behind my reflection in the window. The train stops at Vancouver, crosses the Columbia and Willamette Rivers then slows to enter Portland's Union Station. Gary is waiting on the platform. He scans the train windows looking for me. My stomach twinges with a spasm of guilt and exhilaration.

The width of Gary's lanky body has finally caught up with his height. He is no longer the awkward, out of proportion, baby faced youth. His wiry dark hair cut in a Beatles style along with, bushy eyebrows, and a thick moustache compliment a classic nose and deep pool brown eyes. Tall, dark, and handsome–an apt description.

As I step down from the train our eyes connect. I know what is about to happen, Gary knows what's about to happen. We will drive to Cannon Beach, check into the Tolovana Inn, watch a dazzling sunset as we sip a glass of wine, then sit side by side in front of a comforting fire. Before the evening is over in the name of open marriage I will break my wedding vows.

I can't remember where I heard this–*You don't know you've been eating cheap hamburger until you taste a fine steak.* How true.

"MaryLouise, pass the potatoes! Are you going to let them sit there until they're cold?" The impatient tone of my sister's voice pulls me back to the Christmas dinner table in her dining room surrounded by my extended family.

Judy gives me a penetrating look, "Are you here or off in a daydream?" "Yes, I'm here." I say with a nervous laugh.

If she only knew—I'm right here sitting at this Christmas dinner table between my husband and my lover. Gary's leg is pressed against mine his hand hidden by the tablecloth caresses my thigh. I look around at my mother, father, uncles, aunts, in-laws, and friends. Do they know what is going on under this table? Does the flush on my face reveal the thrill of sitting so close to the man I love?

A few nights later I return to my mother-in-law's apartment, slide between the sheets of my mother-in-law's bed next to my mother-in-law's son trying not to wake him, but the noisy springs of the sagging mattress foil my effort.

Michael stirs, "What time is it?"

"A little after midnight. I'm sorry to be so late. The drive back from Forest Grove took longer than I expected."

Michael moves closer. He is aroused by the thought that an hour ago I left the bed Gary shares with his wife. I'm not interested. My thoughts are on how to bring up the "D" word when we are back home in our apartment in Edmonds.

No one in my family has ever been divorced. No one was ever a Democrat until I left the conservative fold. No one except me drinks. Maybe my aunts and uncles—not my parents, sister, or grandparents. Why has the quiet, shy, responsible member of the family wandered off the path? It is incomprehensible even to me.

"Michael, I need to talk to you about 'us'. Our constant conflict has been on my mind since Christmas. We are both unhappy. I think we need to consider counseling and maybe a divorce." I look over at Michael. He doesn't look as shocked as I expected. "Maybe we should go to a counselor and see what happens. Diane told me about a guy in Seattle."

MY LOVER'S BETRAYAL

I sit in the cold car, stare through fogged windows and heavy March rain at light coming from Gary's apartment. I haven't seen Gary since he moved here two months ago. One lame excuse after another has kept us apart. I told myself he needed space to make difficult decisions. I laughed when he said, "I'm not good for you. I'm full of piss and vinegar." Hints of another relationship have been rationalized and ignored since January. I worried myself into a case of Mono. The reason for the drive to Portland is to know for sure what I don't want to know.

Should I go to the door? Should I leave? I open the car door. I close the car door. If I had a daisy, I could "love me love me not" to the last petal. You drove all the way down here, you might as well humiliate yourself. Just go to the door and confirm what you already know.

The rain soaks me by the time I run from the car to Gary's door. My hand is poised for a few seconds before it knocks hard enough not to be missed. I hear a muffled woman's voice say, "Someone is banging on the door. "Footsteps then the door swings open exposing Gary, trapped between her and me, his face drained of color.

"Hi Gary, I guess you have a roommate."

COMING AROUND FULL CIRCLE

(The healing of my heart and soul.)

1995-2015

Reuniting with My One True Love

Rediscovering my Passion for Creating Beautiful Art

Being Authentic to Myself

Finding Forgiveness and Making Peace with Myself and Others

Seeking Discernment and Wisdom in All Aspects of Life

Spirituality and a Sense of Wonder Reawakens within Me

Seeing and Appreciating the Beauty of the World

A Love for All Creation

WHAT'S ON YOUR LIST TODAY? YOU'LL FIND IT AT FREDDY'S

A narrow gravel path stretches out in front of me. On one side a steep rock face. On the other an abyss. Fear grabs my feet. I turn to my friend Ruth, "I'm going to fall." Ruth reaches her hand out to grasp mine, "Don't worry Mary Louise, we will land safe." Classical music plays softly in the background.

Beeep, beeep, beeep! Jolted awake, my hand knows the switch. With a flick, the alarm stops in mid beep and Portland's "All Classical" announcer stops in mid-sentence. Through a slit in one eye red numbers flash 6:33 on a typical September 1995 Monday morning. I roll over, crack open the other eye. My husband, Richard asleep with his back to me on the other side of our queen size bed, appears unfazed by the alarm. I settle back into the familiar softness of my pillow and comfort of warm flannel sheets. Not a morning person, the early alarm allows time for thoughts to wander while I awaken to the day.

The dream image remains vivid and demands attention. What theme emerges? Fear? Anxiety? How would Carl Jung, the early 20th century Swiss psychiatrist, founder of analytical psychology, and foremost researcher in dream analysis, weigh in? Would Jung view Ruth as the archetypical Wise Old Woman? The thought brings a smile. Ruth is indeed wise, but not old. Christine, a psychologist I've met with for the past year, will propose the person falling and the wise friend represent aspects of me the dreamer. She may also recommend reflection on the dream as a newspaper article in need of a headline. Is this the headline: *Woman Lands Safe Thanks to Her Own Wisdom?*

I hear Richard's even breathing as he sleeps within arms reach unaware of morning, my dream, or me. Would he reject the concept of dream analysis with the same contempt he expressed for psychotherapy last week when I drove him home from work after my appointment with Christine?

"Have you ever thought about sessions with a therapist Richard? You could unload your job frustration."

"I'm not crazy, I don't need therapy."

"This isn't about craziness. Christine says my forty-fifth birthday, this week, places me in the middle of mid-life, a transition akin to the radical changes of puberty. She suggests we are too busy to reflect and see patterns until mid-life."

Richard replies, "The only reason you meet with Christine is to complain about me." Then broods for the remainder of the drive.

Aware of the futility of argument, I drop the subject and use the quiet for my own thoughts. Would it disappoint Richard to know he is seldom a topic of discussion? The conversations with Christine revolve around my life, my patterns. Christine helps me identify patterns, but paths out of those patterns are elusive and scary.

Although I focus on myself with Christine, Richard's suspicions are not unfounded. He and I trudged up two flights of marble steps at the Multnomah County Courthouse for ten years to meet with Mr. Dudley, a family court marriage counselor. The free sessions with Dudley ended two years ago when he retired. We sat side by side in Dudley's small office across from an Escher print of birds turning into fish for uncounted six-week cycles of sessions. He offered us a dependable outlet for our constant conflict about money, a failed business, household duties, and parenting. Responsibility for saving the marriage weighed on Mr. Dudley.

At our last meeting together, instead of Dudley's usual facilitator role, he delivered a fatherly lecture: *You both contribute to the conflict, although Richard maintains greater power by withdrawing. Mary Louise's passionate response to withdrawal feels to Richard like a bulldozer. When Richard closes down, the bulldozer crashes into a stone wall or falls into a bottomless pit. If you want the marriage to succeed, you must work together to find common ground and each agree to meet half way.*

Half way exceeds Richard's capacity. His energy goes to tending deep wounds from a life dominated by parents who prefer his older, smarter, wittier brother. Eighteen years ago common interest in classical music, wine, art, nature, and sex brought us together. Disenchanted with Christian dogma, Richard's strong Jewish identity intrigued me. My spunk and creativity appealed to him. Time revealed the power of dissimilar backgrounds and an opposite approach to life. Richard resigns himself to a glass half-empty. MaryLouise works double time to keep the glass half-full. Christine calls my pattern the superwoman myth.

Richard stirs on his side of our bed then settles onto his back. Except for a full head of dark hair, his short stature, sharp features, and methodical approach to life remind me of my mechanical engineer father. Eighteen years ago, fresh out of a failed marriage to my first husband and failed affair with a life-long friend, Richard provided a safe and dependable outlet for my yearning to love and be loved. Leary of tall, handsome, risk takers like Michael, husband number one, and Gary, friend and lover, I opted for security.

All of a sudden this train of thought crashes into today's date. Damn, today is September 18th. Today is Gary's forty-sixth birthday. Every year on this date, I puzzle through why he left me to marry Shannon and every year I come up with too many missing pieces. I hear my mother's adage, "Don't try to make sense from nonsense," and let the Gary puzzle fade away.

Time to face the day, let go of thoughts, and move into action. Capable of any task, my feet solid against firm bedroom carpet, I draw myself up to all five feet three and one half inches. Not enough chill in the air for a robe over my nightgown, I set out for the stairs. At the top of the stairs an overcast Portland sky, scattered with a hint of blue above billowy thin places, stretches across the full width of two skylights. A circle of cloud softened white light hangs above the Eastern horizon. No time to waste, I descend the stairs to act as alarm clock for the children.

The door at the bottom of the stairs opens into a generous hallway in the center of our late 1930s English style cottage located a half block off NE 33rd Avenue on the wrong side of an arbitrary line between coveted and undesirable neighborhoods. Nine doors and one telephone niche consume every inch of wall in this hallway. To my left: coat closet, utility cupboard, kitchen, our thirteen-year-old son Aaron's room, and the telephone. To my right: living room, linen cupboard, and our five-year-old daughter Rebecca's room. Straight ahead: the bathroom.

I choose Aaron's room first because he is the most difficult to awaken. His door opens to a room characteristic of the delightful resident. Bookshelves are filled with *National Geographic* magazines; geography, astronomy, and biology books; *Donald Duck* and *Scrooge* comics; a full set of *Oz* books and *Sherlock Holmes*. Dinosaurs dot the shelves and animal puppets rest on all surfaces. A telescope mounted on a stand in one corner, a desk piled with writing and art projects along the far wall, the door of an antique oak wardrobe ajar on another wall, the honey colored hardwood floor covered with clothes, a backpack, and more books all signs of an eccentric teenager. To my left, under a navy blue and burgundy flannel duvet Aaron sleeps. The tattered eyelet ruffled edge of a "blankie" peeks out from under his pillow. Children of any age are sweet when asleep.

I dare not use my favorite term of endearment to awaken this boy approaching manhood. "Time to get up Aaron. You have a few minutes. I'll be back." A low groan the only response.

Back into the hall and over to Rebecca's room, her door opens into a cheerful world inhabited by a creative child. In addition to shelves full of stories, ABCs, and counting books, Rebecca's book-cases display dolls, stuffed animals, puzzles, art projects, and ample treasure from Grandmas Beth and Kathryn. Addie, a doll with a brown face and kinky black hair, sleeps in my old doll bunk bed next to an antique oak dresser where the supports for a tall mirror hold a crown of stars on one side and a fluffy magic wand on the other. To my chagrin, Barbie dolls in cheesy outfits stand in front of the mirror. One of those gray areas parents give up, Christine tells me. The heart shaped white iron bed, a gift from Grandma Beth, rests at an angle in one corner on top of Grandma Kathryn's multi-colored Persian design carpet.

Rebecca wrapped in bright pink sheets and a flowered comforter opens her eyes, an eyelet ruffled "blankie" clutched in her hand. I kiss her forehead, "Good morning Sweet Pea."

Rebecca smiles, "Good morning Mama."

"Today is a school day. You need to get up and decide what you want to wear." Knowing Rebecca it will take several outfits before she settles on the perfect ensemble. "I'll come back in a few minutes to see if you need any help."

I hurry back into the hall, past Aaron's room to the kitchen then down the basement stairs alongside Richard's wine cellar, through the playroom, and the laundry room to my office. I find paper and pen, jot down the highlights of my dream, retrieve a shopping list from my drawing table, pick up folded laundry on the way back through the laundry room, and return to main floor bedrooms to check first on Aaron and then Rebecca.

As I enter Aaron's room, he mumbles, "One more minute Mom." To which I reply, "Now Aaron! I'm not leaving this room until you sit up in bed."

My sleepy eyed son, his wavy mullet cut hair curling over the collar of baggy pajamas complies. "OK, I'm up."

"The problem is will you stay up when I leave the room."

"You worry too much Mom."

Aaron's right. Worry, another of my patterns. Aaron's journey through puberty appears less anxiety laden than mine through mid-life.

At the other end of the hall I find Rebecca in her closet. She takes a navy blue jumper off a hanger, "What do you think of this Mama?"

"Looks like a good choice to me. We can tie the new blue ribbon in your hair."

I slide an elastic band off Rebecca's single braid and run my fingers through her silky golden brown waste length hair. "When I come back down from upstairs you need to be dressed so I can brush your hair."

I leave Rebecca in the closet and jog upstairs to dress in the clean clothes retrieved from the laundry room. At the top of the stairs, I poke my head into the study. Richard sits at his desk in robe, pajamas, and leather slippers, a large wine book spread out in front of him and a neat stack of *Wine Spectator* newspapers to one side.

"Are you working ten to seven this week and next?" I ask.

Richard turns toward me, his bottle thick glasses impart a studious air, "Yes and I have an evening wine stewards meeting this Thursday and a tasting next Tuesday." Richard, the Stadium Fred Meyer wine steward, lives and breathes wine.

"Do you remember that my interior design class begins next week? I'm anxious about teaching at the college level for the first time and leaving the children home alone. The class starts at six on Tuesdays and Thursdays? That leaves Aaron to babysit Rebecca and prepare dinner."

"The store manager won't approve a change of schedule and wine tastings are an important part of my job." A defensive tone colors Richard's words.

"Lucky for us Aaron is responsible and enjoys cooking."

An hour later children dressed; hair brushed; pink ribbon tied; hot Wheat Hearts with brown sugar and cream prepared and eaten; dishes stacked; apples, bagels, and cream cheese packed; backpacks ready; list in purse; keys in hand; daughter in tow wearing a pink "I Hiked Mt. Rainier" shirt and black leggings; son missing.

"Where are you Aaron?" I hear footsteps on the dining room floor.

Aaron appears at the kitchen door dressed in Levis and a Bullwinkle sweatshirt, "I was reading this book." He holds up the cover of Dante's *Divine Comedy*, "not only is this a classic, it is fascinating."

Amused I reply, "Astute observation Aaron. Put Hell on hold for now and grab your backpack."

I park my ten-year-old blue Honda Civic in the lot at Broadway Fred Meyer. Mom's taxi delivered Aaron, to eighth grade at Pacific Crest Community School and Rebecca to her all day Kindergarten at Irvington Elementary. A one-stop-shopping expedition then the whole day free to prepare a lesson for the first interior design class. Time for class planning is limited because I promised Tuesday through Thursday to Alice, my best friend and former college roommate. Her office project in Wilsonville is too much for one designer.

I march into the store intent on my list of office supplies and quick fix dinner items for tonight and tomorrow.

Fred Meyer carries everything from soup to nuts and bolts. Their slogan: *What's on your list today? You'll find it at Freddy's.* Local retailer Fred G. Meyer pioneered one-stop-shopping in 1931 when he built the store this enormous new warehouse building replaced. Although I prefer to shop at Natures, the locally owned natural food store, sometimes convenience and an employee discount compel me to wink at principles.

My first destination, the office supply section in the middle of the building between housewares and grocery. The generic product selection relieves me of decision stress. I pick up two black three ring binders, two sets of clear tab dividers, and a package of page protectors. This should be enough to organize the first weeks of my class. Binders, dividers, and protectors in hand, I turn the corner into a main aisle headed for the grocery section.

A familiar figure catches my eye and directs my attention across to the opposite aisle. Recognition of the unmistakable six-foot-seven height of an attractive man walking my way from between two long rows of American Greetings cards sends a wave of anxiety over me. This is the man I remembered earlier this morning, the former friend, former lover who dumped me. With time to scoot back into the office supply aisle before discovery, I perform a quick mental check of my appearance. A new youthful short haircut, stylish Eddie Bauer shirt, slim cropped pants, and saltwater sandals boost my confidence. Although temped to escape, curiosity holds me fast.

I blurt out the first words that enter my head, "Happy Birthday Gary!"

Gary's lanky body stops in mid stride. He turns wide eyes in my direction, his dark eyebrows raised in an expression suggestive of a surprised cartoon character. His moustache moves. His mouth opens. No words emerge.

Obligated to fill the silence while he attempts to regain his composure, I say, "So what have you been up to for the last eighteen years?"

Hope for retribution is dashed when he regains his voice, "I'm still married to Shannon. We have an eleven-year-old son." He pauses, checks for a reaction then continues, "I work in securities."

I remember his police work and stints in security with the Port of Portland and Intel. "Are you still a security guard?"

"No, I buy and sell securities for clients with a minimum of $50,000 to invest."

I notice long arms extended beyond the cuffs of a rumpled blue-gray tweed sports jacket and well-worn athletic shoes on size fifteen feet. I wonder how many clients have entrusted their life savings.

"What about you Mary Louise?" he asks.

"My husband and I have two children a boy thirteen and a girl five. I drove them to school then stopped here to pick up some supplies for the class I teach at Portland Community College." Revealing details of my life weakens my confidence. I regret my decision to engage in this awkward conversation. Glancing at my watch, "Sorry, no time to talk. Goodbye Gary." I turn the corner and dart into the closest aisle. Gary is frozen in place.

The list forgotten, I speed shop a few essentials and join the "under ten items" queue. Across the store near the door, Gary scans lines of shoppers. I duck down behind the gum and candy display, pay for my purchases, and follow a long route out to the parking lot to avoid detection.

Course syllabus, lecture notes, *Inside Today's Home* textbook, slides, slide projector, and three ring binders, cover every surface in my eight by ten basement office. A small window high on one wall gives a worm's eye view of clearing sky. No clearing for me today. On the drive home from Fred Meyer a knot formed in my stomach while a storm of Gary memories brewed in my mind. We shared every major life event from early childhood through high school, college, and into our twenties. Our passionate affair at the end of my first marriage dissolved into a state of confusion then he married Shannon and disappeared. I wrapped hurt and humiliation in an impenetrable cocoon of anger to remain safe. Three months later I met Richard.

Fingers type an outline on the computer while my mind wanders to a list of family and friends searching for a safety valve to process the encounter with Gary this morning. I tick off the reactions – confusion, reprimand, betrayal, condemnation, worry, and disappointment. Without a viable outlet and a deadline to meet, I wrap more silk around the cocoon and let go of Gary memories for the second time today.

By evening, I am desperate to tell someone about the chance meeting at the store. Dinner over, dishes done, Rebecca tucked into bed and Aaron listening to music, I stop by the open bathroom door where Richard brushes his teeth.

In a quasi-casual voice, I say to him, "You'll never guess who I ran into at the Broadway Fred Meyer this morning."

"If I'll never guess, why don't you tell me?"

"Gary Howarth."

"Who?"

"You remember me talking about Gary, the old boyfriend who ditched me."

"Oh, you mean the jerk. Did you create a scene?"

"No, not in a public place. Get this, Gary told me he invests money for people. I wouldn't trust him with the pennies in my piggy bank."

THE JOURNEY THAT REUNITED MARY LOUISE AND GARY AND THEIR DEEP LOVE

On Friday, four days after the incident at Fred Meyer, a small envelope addressed in Gary's familiar angled script arrives in my mail box. Large letters read, *Mary Louise,* no last name, no return address. I peer out the living room window into the warm Indian Summer afternoon. How did Gary find me? Is he out there in his car watching me?

The note in my mailbox reminds me of a phone call from Gary in 1980 two years after he married Shannon. The call surprised me because it was the first contact in two years, my phone number was new and unlisted. Richard and I bought this house in January and the phone call was in February.

The phone rings, "Hello."

"Hello MaryLouise, this is Gary."

I sit down on the side of the bed across from myself reflected in the wardrobe mirror. How did he find me? "What do you want?"

"I just wanted to say hello. It has been a long time since we talked. I wondered if we could get together sometime."

"I have made a life for myself. We have nothing to talk about Gary." After the call I wonder if my prediction came true and he is miserable. I guess I will never know.

Hesitant to open the small note sized envelope, I reflect on the inner turmoil created by my short conversation with Gary on

144

Monday. My life although far from perfect, is predictable. Will this note upset my equilibrium? Fear and curiosity live side by side.

Once again, curiosity triumphs. I slit open the envelope and slide out the American Greetings' note card decorated with an Impressionist watercolor of red poppies. As I unfold the note, an "Investment Representative" business card with Gary's name, Clackamas, Oregon address, and phone number falls into my hand. Inside Gary's handwritten phrases sting rather than sooth.

"I enjoyed our visit."

What visit? You were speechless and I disappeared before you could recover enough to engage me in conversation.

"Lunch and free investment information."

Not on your life buddy! I trusted you eighteen years ago. I'm not stupid enough to do it again.

"Warmest Regards,"

How can you pretend a regard as warm or otherwise? You toyed with my affection abandoned me without an explanation. Did I expect an apology? No time for this nonsense, I close the note, push it back into the envelope, and toss it into a basket of bills on the kitchen counter. Is the trash a better choice? Then life happens—kids, work, therapy, car accident, scary dream about death, holidays, freezing temps followed by a hundred-year flood, visitors from Russia.

Gary slipped back into a category of risky subjects too painful to remember.

February 7, 1996

A business envelope addressed in Gary's angled script to *Mary Louise,* no last name, arrives in the mailbox five months later. I turn it over in my hand, notice the Clackamas, Oregon post office box in the return address, ponder Gary's motive then drop the letter unopened into a basket of bills on the kitchen counter. A day or two passes, then a week, a month. For a while I pretend not to notice then I forget. Meals prepared, dishes done, bills piled on, the envelope waits.

March 4, 1996

As I sort through March bills and bank statements, Gary's letter appears in my hand. I stare at *Mary Louise* written on the envelope. A moment of curiosity prods me to turn it over a run my finger under the flap and pull out the single sheet of pale gray lined paper. The paper falls open, a long overdue handwritten apology unfolds. "I make no excuses, acknowledge mistakes, apologize for the hurt...I've changed, I miss being your friend. Best Regards, Gary...P.S. Don't feel any obligation to reply, but if you do I can be reached at...post office box #499."

Instead of satisfaction, Gary's letter unleashes fury. I stomp down the stairs to my basement office, park myself in front of the computer and bang out a response.

> "You have changed. I find that difficult to believe. Once I have been deceived, I am hesitant to be caught again. It is the fact that you were dishonest with me that angered me the most. You had a wife and at least two girlfriends. Your dishonesty makes me angry. My gullibility makes me angry. I am not proud of my behavior. I hurt other people and acted in poor taste. Your rejection was beneficial because our relationship wasn't right for me. I have no regrets about leaving Michael. Maybe it required drastic measures for me to see that I was dead in that relationship. I have learned a lot since then and I have a lot to learn. I am a strong and independent person. I define myself by who I am, not by who I am with. My life is full, some good, some not so good. I'm not sure what you wanted to accomplish by contacting me and I am not sure what I want to accomplish by responding. I hope your life is all you want it to be."
>
> Mary Louise

The moment the printer spits out my rant I fold it, stuff it in an envelope addressed to P. O. Box #499, smash a stamp onto the comer and stomp back up the stairs to find my coat. I rush out the door, down to the comer, and my hands drops the letter in the mail box. As the envelope slides slowly down the blue metal shoot into the darkness and the flap closes with a clunk, my anger dissipates. A sick feeling of regret for my impulsiveness? Gary, adverse to conflict, will read my letter and that will be the end of it. What if he no longer checks this post office box?

I compose and mail a second note, "Even though I'm still angry, maybe we could have lunch"

March 1996

A few days later the phone rings- Gary's voice on the other end of the line. We talked for over an hour and we agreed to meet for lunch.

THE LUNCH

April 9, 1996

I t took hours to make certain every detail of my appearance was perfect the day of our lunch and to show him what he missed.

The following is a conversation Norman the angel has prior to our lunch and then the conversation Gary and I have.

"This is your last chance Norman. Get this couple together or you're demoted."

"It isn't my fault boss. They're both dense. The first time around she thought the right guy was too tall and too goofy. She fell head over heals for his best friend. What was I to do?"

"Yes, I know. Some people take longer than others to learn what they want in life. She needed that first relationship to sort herself out."

"The second time he was the one hell bent on screwing up the opportunity I gave him to make things right. She told him he would be sorry for dumping her to marry that other woman, but oh no, he knew better."

"The fact that he got drunk on a pitcher of margaritas is no excuse for letting him fly to Reno for midnight nuptials. Come on Norman, a poodle as the witness?"

"I thought it might help with an annulment."

"Well, your plan fell through. They stayed married and had a son together."

"Not until after they separated for two years. He called her then hoping to reconnect, but he never got around to telling her she was right, that he was sorry. She hung up on him."

"Do you blame her? She just bought a house with a man and they were trying to make a life together."

"OK, OK you're right you're always right. She used her anger as a shield. I didn't realize she was going for safety. I thought the guy I put in her path that time would be too much like her father. Not her typical tall, dark, and handsome risk taker."

"Your plan backfired Norman. You can't get it right. Now she has two children."

"And ten years of marriage counseling. The only reason they stopped going two years ago was because the counselor retired."

"Don't hold her responsible. Give her credit for trying to make your mistake work."

"Do I get points for my Fred Meyer trick last September? Do you know how hard it was after eighteen years to get both of them to the same place at the same time...on his birthday no less? It was a perfect drama. She wished him 'Happy Birthday.' He almost fainted."

"I have to admit that was an impressive move, but she was still so angry she almost scooted down a side aisle."

"Yeah, I was sweating."

"Then you failed to intervene when she tossed the note he sent as a first attempt to invite her to lunch. Four months later she almost ignored his letter of apology. That was some reply she decided to put together. No man in his right mind would respond to a letter like that not even this hapless fellow. What did you do to change her mind about lunch?"

"As soon as she saw her letter slide down the mailbox chute she was sorry for her hot-headed rejection. That's when I planted the idea of a follow up note to the effect – *I think you're a jerk, but I'll agree to lunch*. I got lucky. She still loves him."

"Which is why this has to work this time. They love each other and they're both miserable."

"I'll give it my best boss, but my control of the situation is limited. All I can do is nudge. What if he comes across as insincere? What if she decides he can't be trusted?"

"The fact that some cases are more difficult is why I give you three chances. No excuses this time. Get to work Norman."

I swing the door of Papa Hayden's open to reveal Gary, dressed in a navy-blue suit and black athletic shoes, seated on a bench waiting for me. He pretends to read the Wall Street Journal his eyes more on me walking through the door than the paper. His stare of approval – sweet revenge.

"Hi Gary, have you waited long?"

"I was beginning to think you changed your mind about lunch. Are there any rotten tomatoes in your purse?"

"I make no promises."

The hostess ushers us to a table in a corner by the grill. I position myself so that light from the front windows flatters. Gary, across the table, appears more put together than before. His hair, still black with no sign of gray, is combed back in a style more sophisticated than his old boyish side part and untamed cowlicks. The neat black moustache and soft brown eyes, are unchanged. The total effect is middle-aged, charming businessman.

"Are you paying for lunch? Seems like you owe me." I say.

"Yes, order anything you like." We both order Caesar salad with chicken. Not because we plan to eat. I suspect he is too nervous to do more than copy me. I have him just where I want him.

"Tell me about your son. Is he as crazy as you were?"

Gary laughs. His smile turns a light on in his eyes. "He is a character. We have fun together. Last week he dressed up as Tolkien for a school project. How about your children."

"I love them dearly and at the same time raising children is the hardest thing I've ever done."

"Wow, it is the easiest for me."

"Yeah, that sounds like a guy your wife must do all the heavy lifting."

"No, I get Gary ready for school and spend time with him"

He shares stories about where he has lived- Oregon to Colorado to Ohio to New York to Southern California to Oregon to Washington and back to Oregon.

"I've been in the same house for 14 years."

I notice Gary staring at me and smiling. "It seems like no time has passed and I've missed our conversations."

"And who is to blame for that."

"I am."

"It has never made sense to me. You hung around for years and then as soon as I responded you disappeared."

"I was thinking with the wrong part of my anatomy."

"That's for sure."

"I loved you for all the right reasons MaryLouise."

I look around to see if anyone is listening to our conversation.

"What do you mean?"

"I always admired you for your intellect, wisdom, and compassion. Did you know that your father came to see me at work, at Intel? How did he know?"

"Judy told my parents. I trusted her and she betrayed my trust."

"He told me to leave you alone. He said I was messing up your life".

Gary pays the check with cash.

"May I walk you to your car?"

Turns out my car is parked behind his.

I feel the chemistry between us but we never touch.

I follow him around the block back to Milwaukie Blvd. He turns right, I turn left. I'm churned up inside. Will I ever see him again?

DIFFERENT THIS TIME AROUND

66 "The relationship is different than before, no lost sleep this time around."

If I say those words out loud, will they silence the voice in my head determined to annoy me while I fuss with my hair and agonize over what to wear today? My husband, thirteen-year-old son and five-year-old daughter left for work and school an hour ago. Since then, I cleaned the kitchen, made the beds, and put away the laundry.

"Wait a minute. What do you mean no lost sleep this time? After lunch with Gary a week ago, you got up in the middle of the night to write him a letter because you couldn't sleep."

"No, it was the chocolate in the leftover desert I brought home from lunch with him at Papa Haydn's that kept me awake. Might as well use the time to write a thank you note for lunch. I was clear about my priorities. Gary knows I don't want to disturb my life. He feels the same. "

"So, what is your excuse for telling him in the note that if he wants to befriends again he needs to know that you still love him? You invited him to your house. What were you thinking?"

Nothing wrong with an expression of honest feelings. We were good friends once. We can be friends again. There is no better way to know who I am than to see my home."

"Even though this guy dumped you eighteen years ago to marry the woman he is still married to, you think you can trust him."

"I told him how much his actions hurt and humiliated me. He apologized. Maybe we were incompatible life partners, but that doesn't mean we can't be friends."

"So, does anyone know about his visit this morning?"

152

"I told Richard about the lunch last week. Gary is an old friend. We are renewing a friendship? Quiet, I hear the doorbell."

"Yeah, I know. Your stomach did a flip-flop. By the way, you look terrific in those black leggings. Good plan to cover a few too many home-made cookies with a big sweater."

My feet race down the stairs to the living room. The bell rings again. I fumble with the deadbolt key then take a cleansing breath to calm myself before I swing back the heavy front door

"Hi Gary, welcome to my home."

Gary stands on my porch in the same navy blue suit and the same black athletic shoes he wore to lunch. He ducks to avoid brushing his head against the awning. "Nice to see you again, MaryLouise." He shifts back and forth from one foot to the other unsure about his next move.

Now that he is here on the porch, my brain freezes, "Come in," is all I can manage.

Given permission to enter, Gary strides into the living room. "Nice house. I can see your touch. The leaded glass window is beautiful."

His comment provides a safe topic, "We bought the house because of the front window and the knights on the tile around the hearth. The place was a nightmare of gold, green, and orange when we moved in. I did most of the work myself. A carpenter friend helped me finish the basement and upstairs. It took nine years of weekend projects. Would you like to see the house?"

Gary nods his head, "Your note promised a tour. Didn't you say your life is in this house?"

He corners me with my own words,

"Yes, home is my sanctuary and the objects I collect hold my stories." I walk Gary past my grandmother's table in the dining room to the kitchen where children's artwork and photos cover the refrigerator. I take him downstairs to see piles of projects in my art-space, the playhouse I built for my daughter in the family room. Back to the main floor for a peek into my son's room filled with books and my daughter's room populated by stuffed animals, dolls, and puppets.

We end up in the central hall where one of seven doors leads upstairs to the bedroom shared with my husband. The voice attempts to stop me, *"Are you sure this is a good idea?"* I open the door and start up the stairs. *"Oh no, too late now."*

"Previous owners roughed in two rooms up here. The stairs were carpeted with orange shag. The bedroom carpet was turquoise. I reframed the rooms and had skylights installed." We reach the bedroom where my white iron bed dominates more than I remember. Gary fidgets next to me. I sweep my arm like a real estate agent showing a house, "Here is the master bedroom, over here the bath, and a study behind this wall." Then I retreat down the stairs with Gary close behind. I wonder if the heat I feel under my sweater shows up red on my face.

"Do you mind if I use your phone? I need to check on an appointment." Gary asks as we enter the kitchen.

"The phone is over there on the counter I'll wait for you in the living room." I'm happy for a chance to cool off in private.

Gary makes several calls. From what I hear of the one-sided conversations, his work life is as chaotic as it was eighteen years ago.

After the last call he moves toward me in the living room. His eyes glisten with tears. Surprised by the sudden show of emotion I ask, "Is there a problem?"

"No, I'm overwhelmed by seeing you again. I've missed you MaryLouise." "I've missed you too Gary. May I give you a hug?"

He opens his arms to me, bends down, and tries to touch my forehead with his lips. I turn my head give him a quick squeeze and pull away to the other side of the room. "Come sit on the sofa so we can talk about old times."

Gary pauses with his arms still in a hug position as though he failed to notice my maneuver then he walks to the sofa, arranges his lanky body at the end closest to my perch on a nearby chair.

I steer the conversation away from my discomfort to memories of teenage escapades, stories about his son and my two children, and questions about his life for the past two decades.

Gary's deep brown eyes connect with mine, tears spill down his cheeks. I reach over; place my hand on his knee. "Did I upset you?

"No, just the opposite. The truth is I've never been close to many people in my life. I value your friendship because I can talk to you." Gary takes my hand, pulls me over to the sofa. I allow him to place a gentle kiss on my lips right there in front of the garage door sized leaded glass window facing the whole neighborhood. A tingle ripples from my lips to the knot in my stomach.

This time Gary pulls back, "I'm sorry, I have to go. May I see you again?" He rushes ahead without waiting for an answer. "Would you enjoy a walk at the Rhododendron Garden? It should be in full bloom. How about Thursday morning at ten?"

"I shouldn't, but I will." I reply as he moves to the door. Then Gary is gone, out the door, down the steps.

I lean my back against the front door, the weight of my body pushes until the latch clicks. "Shit, now what?"

"Hmm, no lost sleep this time? Go ahead, look for the Roberta Flack album."

I flip through albums in search of one avoided for years. A familiar cover falls into view. I slide the record out, place it on the turntable, gently drop the needle, and turn the volume up until the heartbeat rhythm of "First Time Ever I Saw Your Face" throbs in my body. I want to lose myself in the music, ignore the question shouted in my head. *"You dipped your toe in the river. Do you know how to swim?"*

Five months later, eleven days before Gary's next birthday, we were married.

REFLECTIONS OF OUR TIME AT THE RHODODENDRON GARDEN

I am so much in love with you. It's January 9, 2001 and I said that to him this morning. I thought of it in the night. I almost woke him up to tell him.

Sleeping together, feeling our bodies touch, and becoming one. It is the best thing in life- a perpetual sleepover with my best friend. We have a ritual of various positions moving from each to the next as we fall asleep tight together.

Sometimes he twitches, jerking his arm. Sharp elbows. I stay close as long as I can. The jerks wake me up, but I don't mind. Being close is all that matters.

What is that draws us to each other? What force made this happen? Why didn't it happen before? Why couldn't we have been the only?

I am drawn to him. Alice says we are like dogs in heat. It isn't that. It's as if the two of us were meant to be joined as one.

These thoughts bring back memories of the Rhododendron Garden which was our third encounter in 1996.

I have never been so close to anyone as I was to Gary that day. The power of our closeness was like a magnet drawing us together. Bonding us to each other.

We barely spoke. We stood under a tree canopy with our arms entwined for what seemed like forever. Under the trees we looked out at the water and the beauty of the garden as rain filtered down. It was as though everything in the world had stopped and there was only the two of us standing there twined together my back against his chest his arms wrapped around mine, his hand resting in mine.

I remember the color of his shirt and tie and how his jacket brought out the orange gold in his tie. I remember how the soft suede made my skin tingle.

We were closer to each other than any two beings could be as we stood as one like the trees around us silent, calm, strong, separate from reality.

I was more vulnerable than I have ever been and without the distraction of a kiss.

I hold the picture of that day engraved on my mind forever. I hold the memory of our oneness forever a part of my soul.

As I left I knew I had to decide or maybe I already decided. I just needed to see what I had already done.

I went home and got out the collection of Robert Frost poems Gary had given me in 1976 when we were "in love" twenty years before. I read the Road Not Taken and knew a second chance to try the other path was rare, to take the *"one less traveled by, and that has made all the difference"*. I had to take the leap; I had to try the road. I had to see where it would go. I decided to kiss him.

DANGEROUS PURSUIT

Gravel flies as Gary backs the car out of a deserted parking area along a dark forested section of the Washington Park road between the Rose Garden and the Portland Zoo. It is after ten. Like middle-aged teenagers necking in the back seat of a car–more than an hour was swept away by passion.

"Are you sure the park closes at ten. Do they actually lock a gate?"

"We'll soon find out." Gary replies while navigating the car around the last hairpin curve before the Rose Garden.

The headlights shine on two white metal arms meeting in the middle of our path to safety. "I guess that answers my question about the gate." A sick feeling grabs my stomach. Thoughts of how to explain a night spent in Washington Park or a late-night walk out of here race through my mind.

Gary spins the wheel into a sudden U-turn well before reaching the barrier. "I don't remember a gate at the zoo end of the road. It won't take long to see if we can go out that way. I'm sorry I put you in this predicament Mary Louise. I lost track of time."

Minutes pass in silence. Red reflectors on two arms of a closed gate appear in front of us. A padlock dangles from the overlap where the arms meet securing them to each other. We are caught in a trap of our own making.

I lead a double life. In one life I am wife to an intractable husband, mother of two delightful children, daughter of aging parents, sister, aunt, niece, friend. In the other life I am involved in an affair with Gary, a lifelong friend and former lover.

This double life threatens everything I care about. My fourteen-year-old son Aaron and six-year-old daughter Rebecca are the center of my world. Whether or not I continue the affair, seek a divorce, or end the affair and remain miserable in my marriage, my actions put them in peril.

In spite of the inability to solve our problems after ten years of on and off marriage counseling, I made a promise to my husband that I have broken. He deserves better.

I am immune to my father's opinion because he is unhappy no matter what I do, but how will my ailing mother deal with the knowledge that her forty-five-year-old daughter is pursuing another childish dream? I already used my free pass when I had an affair and divorced my first husband eighteen years ago. Will friends and family understand my search for happiness? To lose the love and respect of the people who mean the most to me will leave a hole in my heart.

This affair with Gary is risky. He dumped me to marry another woman eighteen years ago. Will Gary abandon me again or will he walk away from his wife and turn his twelve-year-old son's life upside down like his parents' divorce did to him at the same age. Is this affair an idle pastime or a quest for lasting love?

Another U-turn, more flying gravel. Gary's long ago police academy training kicks in. He chases back down the road as though after a suspect. There is no one else in sight. We are the only lawbreakers.

The Rose Garden gate appears again. Gary stops the car and looks over at me, "Maybe it isn't locked."

Fueled by an adrenalin rush I sprint from the car to the obstacle that blocks our way. The long metal arm gives when I touch it. We are safe.

FIRST TIME AT NINA'S (GARY'S MOTHER) APARTMENT

L ife laughs at plans. I plot a flawless strategy for the day then life hits me with an

unexpected joke. This morning is a perfect example.

I open the door to my middle school aged son's room. "Time to get up Aaron."

Aaron groans, "My stomach is queasy. I can't go to school today?"

"Maybe you will feel better if you get up."

"No, I need to go back to sleep." He pulls the covers over his head. Experience tells me argument is futile.

On to six-year-old Rebecca's room, "Wake up Sweet Pea, it's a school day."

Rebecca sneezes, "My nose is plugged up. I don't feel good. Can I stay home from school?"

What are the chances both children wake up sick on the same day? My plan for the day is canceled.

My husband left for work a few minutes ago. My children, Aaron an eighth grader and his six year old sister Rebecca, are home sick today. In a few minutes my lover will call. My plan was to verify that he can come by to pick me up for our date at his mother's apartment...

In a few minutes my lover will call from the service station on the comer to make sure the family is gone so he can pick me up to spend the day with him at his elderly mother's apartment. He has already driven her to the Lloyd Center armed with enough money to shop, buy lunch, and take in a movie.

JOURNEY TO WHOLENESS

My emotional healing began when Gary reentered my life in the spring of 1996 and we were married on September 7th, 1996. I discovered what it felt like to be truly loved and accepted as I Am. Not only accepted, but cherished and embraced as a special and unique individual. We were both able to put aside our egos and baggage and love each other more than ourselves. Few people know what it's like for someone to care more about you than himself or herself. Gary was one of the few people in my life who ever really "got" me and encouraged me to be who I am without any false pretenses. I felt at peace, secure, and loved. We were always meant to be together, we both commented that the Universe was back in proper alignment. Why did it take so long for both of us to realize this? Don't misinterpret this; there were still many issues and challenges that I would face; however this was the start of coming around full circle.

One of the most difficult challenges was my mother's illness and death. In August 2000, her health began to deteriorate again and this time there was nothing the doctors could do. No one knew how long it would be, maybe a few weeks, maybe a few months. At the end of August a Hospice nurse began visiting Mother at home every few days. I returned to Bainbridge so I could help Rebecca prepare for the start of a new school year, leaving Mother in the care of my sister and my three aunts. By Friday of the first week of school, it was clear that Mother's time was even shorter than we thought. I returned to Portland knowing that although it was important to be with her it was going to be excruciating.

One of the complications I dreaded was the life-long tension between my sister, Judy, and myself. We are as different as night and day with almost nothing in common. Over the months of Mother's illness we had been getting along fairly well because there was so much to do. We could divide up the tasks and pretty much stay out of each other's way. On the morning after I arrived back in Portland, I decided to take Judy aside to tell her how much I didn't want to be there. We looked into each other's eyes and both realized we had found a common bond, our love for our mother and our fear of her death. We held each other in silence just as Mother had so often done and we each knew all we could do was be together. Later that day we shared our fears with a family member. He said, "you are giving her a gift, you are helping her die gracefully." No matter how hard it was to be there, it was a gift we both wanted to give.

We took turns sitting with her day and night. We didn't always know how to care for her, but did our best. One time when it took Judy, my three aunts and me fifteen minutes to turn her and make her comfortable again we thought we must look like a comedy routine, but mother said, "You are doing a remarkable job."

On the morning mother died I had been up with her almost all night and I needed comfort so I opened *The Cup of Our Life*. The page I found was *The Gift of Be-ing*. **"Just to be is a blessing, just to live is holy."** I thought about the long hours of sitting with Mother holding her hand. It didn't feel like enough, but be-ing with her was all I could offer.

The night before had been difficult. Mother was suffering even though we had given her morphine. Once, while I was lying next to her, she stopped breathing. I thought she was gone so I said "I love you" and suddenly she started breathing again. When I shared this with the Hospice nurse in the morning, she said she thought Mother was having a hard time letting go. She said, "It would be a blessing for you to leave the room and let her go."

So we turned off the soft music, closed the blinds, told her we loved her, said goodbye, and left the room. We were in agony. My sister deals with anxiety by talking so she went off to call someone on the phone. I wish I could say I sat down and quietly meditated, but that is not what I did. Instead, I paced around the living room making a large circuit that ended every few rounds with a peak around the partly opened door to Mother's room. What seemed like a lifetime was really only 15 or 20 minutes. The next time when I approached the door I could tell her labored breathing had stopped and she was gone.

Before I had a chance to absorb the magnitude of what had just happened, my dearest friend Alice appeared at the door. She said, "I had a feeling you needed me this morning so I came as quickly as I could." She wrapped me in her arms and held me close while we rocked back and forth crying.

The day of mother's memorial service Judy asked if I would like to have Mother's necklace with the letter "B". It is a "B" for Bethine, my mother's name. I started wearing it because it made me feel closer to her. One day a friend asked about the necklace and when I told her why I wore it, she suggested it could also remind me to just be. When I touch it I think about my mother's gift of be-ing with me.

Mother always wanted my Sister and I have to have a good relationship and our shared experience of taking care of our Mother was the beginning of our healing. However after my Mother's death I descended into a deep depression and could find little solace because of the grief I was experiencing.

My relationship with my Father was another issue that bubbled up to the surface after Mother's death. For many reasons I never felt close to him and this was exacerbated by his actions during and after Mother's death. During my Mother's illness my Father expressed no compassion for his wife with whom he had spent 50 years. After her death he immediately started looking for a replacement.

A grief counselor helped me sort out my feelings and look at my Father objectively. I discovered that he suffers from an undiagnosed developmental disorder called Asperger's Syndrome. With regard to my Mother's death it is a loss I must live with and will deeply miss her for the remainder of my life. Through doubt and despair comes life and joy. As Abraham Lincoln once said, "Sorrow comes to all…. Perfect relief is not possible, except with time. You cannot now realize that you will ever feel better…. and yet…you are sure to be happy again." My journey of healing and wholeness continues.

GARY HOWARTH'S THOUGHTS CONCERNING MARY LOUISE

My wife descended into a deep depression because of the death of her mother and issues with her father. However, as time passed and with a great deal of work on her part I began to notice a change. Mary Louise has an indomitable spirit and a healing took place. What emerged was a new burst of creative energy.

Being an artist has always been a large part of her life, and making beautiful art gave her tremendous satisfaction and joy. She was also passionate about life and making a difference in the World. Once she was committed to a project there was no stopping her, she did everything at least 200%.

Mary Louise played a pivotal role in establishing an arts education program in schools. She worked for a year to produce 20 colored pencil drawings for a one-person art show at the Bainbridge Library. She collaborated with a writer and genealogist to teach a series of memoir classes. She established an art docent resource center.

Mary Louise was a mentor for her daughter's 18th century dress making project. She engaged in family research including talking to the sole survivor of the plane crash that took Joe's life. She took a job as a volunteer coordinator for a nine-branch library system then moved into the role of facilities manager. At the library she occasionally had an alternative personality named Dottie Mae. Dottie Mae gave hilarious presentations at staff meetings.

There is no one quite like Mary Louise she had such tenacity and a drive to do the right thing and help correct problems she observed.

LEADER OF THE TEAM, KITSAP REGIONAL LIBRARY FACILITIES MANAGER

I t's Sunday morning, the phone rings. Maybe I won't answer, then I notice the name on the caller ID–it's one of the library directors. I tick off a mental list of every possible disaster related to Friday's furniture installation in Circulation and Collection Management including the obvious tension between Sue and Leif the facilities manager.

"Hello this is Sue, I hate to bother you on the weekend so I'll get right to the point. Leif is on leave for a while. Do you think you could supervise the remodeling project at the Sylvan Way Library?" A wave of anxiety washes over me. Despite my qualifications, do I want this headache? "Yes, I can manage the project." I hear myself say. "Great! I'll see you in the morning and we'll talk about the details. First thing tomorrow, I will introduce your new role to the team."

The team–my mind flashes to an onsite inspection many years ago when a contractor whistled at me from the top of a ladder, "Yur the purtiest little architect I've ever seen." He stopped whistling when I told him the veneer skins on thirty recently installed doors were rotary cut not plain sliced as called for in the specification.

I also replay the countless times my non-handy husband Gary has come along to the lumberyard merely to provide muscle and the guy at the counter looks past me to him, "what can I do for you today sir?" Unfazed I rattle off my list while Gary wanders over to the popcorn cart, "Six eight foot 2 x 4

165

studs, a bundle of 12" stakes, four bags of Quikrete and these lag bolts. I'll go out to the yard and pick the lumber myself to avoid garbage like the last time."

Although I was a quiet child, happier playing alone with my dolls than venturing out into the world, I come from a deep well of independent women. Mother never let gender specific labels deter her. I can still see her running back and forth across the front lawn behind a power mower while the neighbor ladies peek at her through tilted Venetian blinds. My mother's mother grew up in mining camps where she learned self-reliance. When her husband was called back to Montana one summer to help his family with ranching duties, Grandma preached at the church he served in a small Illinois town. Members of the congregation were overheard saying, "The lady is a better preacher than the man." My grandmother's mother, born in Maine and raised on the Montana prairie, worked as a post-mistress to support her nine children when her blacksmith husband died.

Back to the problem at hand, how did I get myself into this mess? A few weeks after accepting a half time volunteer coordinator job at the nine-branch rural library district in our county, co-workers began talking about an upcoming remodel of the library service center. After thirty frustrating years in commercial interior design I was ready to try a new career, but sitting there at my desk in the middle of the chaotic office I wondered if it would be more painful to watch the project unfold or offer my help. I chose the latter. Eighteen months later the first phase of a three-phase project is nearly finished with a fast approaching project completion date only two months away.

I spend the remainder of the day doing what I always do in a daunting situation, over prepare. Beginning with an assessment of the unpalatable issues dished onto my plate and then moving on to creating a plan for Monday, my biggest concern is supervising an all-male team consisting of two in-house facilities staff members, Terry and Rory, augmented by a variety of casual laborers and sub-contractors. They spend more time standing around talking than they devote to getting the job done.

Monday morning came early following a restless night of adding items to the list. I walk into the conference room prepared and confident on the outside—Jell-O on the inside. Sue gives the guys some background and then introduces me. They all know my other hats, volunteer coordinator and designer, but they don't know me. Deciding to jump right in, "My extensive hands-on construction experience doesn't mean I have all the answers. If I tell you to do something one way and you have a better idea, let me know. I don't want to waste anyone's time. I also expect high quality work so we can take pride in the finished product. We will meet every morning to go over a list for the day."

I hand out my list, assign tasks, answer questions,and then everyone goes to work. Much to my surprise, we all survive the first day. I spend the evening making a new list of projects for Tuesday because the team has already blasted through the first one.

Tuesday morning when I pull up to the curb behind the heating contractor's truck, I notice a ladder leaning against the building. Until this moment, I never considered the fact that my new role would require going up on the roof. "No time like the present," my mother would say. While the women in Technical Services peek through the blinds, I reach down and pull the back of my skirt between my legs, carefully climb, up the ladder, step warily off onto the slope of the roof, find the contractor in the mechanical room, then retrace my route back to solid ground, all without killing or exposing myself. Terry and Rory meet me at the bottom of the ladder and I can see my stock just went up on the market of male opinion.

Over the next week I discover the guys aren't slackers at all. They wanted to work; no one gave them anything to do. Day after day they gobble up Lists of tasks like candy and beg for more. They call me boss and get a kick out of observing reactions when they point and say, "Don't look at us, she's in charge."

Two months pass. The project is almost complete. One day. Terry and Rory ask me to come with them to see the finishing touches in a new conference room. As we walk into the room, Rory apologizes because the white board is mounted off center due to the heater location, "We know it isn't up to your standards, but we did our best." Touched and grateful I say, "It's perfect."

SPIRITUAL JOURNEY

In my late twenties, years before Gary and I got back together I was done with religion. My first marriage to a seminary student and a number of bad experiences in the church, this one and others, soured me on church and I could no longer pretend to believe the new testament stories about angels and miracles I grew up with. I began to explore Judaism about the same time I met my second husband a secular Jew.

Less than a year after we were married Gary took a job in the Seattle area and we moved to Bainbridge Island. He had lived there a few years previous and attended Rolling Bay Presbyterian Church. He asked me to go to church with him. I was still leery of church and religion, but as a love thing I agreed to go with him except on communion Sundays. The first Sunday we were there was communion. In fact it seemed that every time we went they served communion. I sat in the pew while Gary went forward. I had a problem with communion and didn't participate. The music was beautiful, the sermon were moving and the people welcoming. We became involved in cooking for more than 100 people at an after school program for families on Wednesday afternoon and evening.

In February or March every year the women of the church went away for a weekend retreat. Gary nudged me to sign up. "Doesn't a week-end away from the family sound like fun? He asked. "You'll have a chance to meet some new people."

Somewhat reluctantly I carpooled to the retreat center with some of the people we cooked with on Wednesdays.

I did meet some wonderful people and had a great weekend in spite of the fact that the speaker had a meltdown and left on Saturday night. The drama brought the group closer together. On Sunday morning the retreat was to close with a worship service. I sat toward the back because I knew communion would be part of the service. Before communion was served Bev, the spiritual director on staff at the church, blessed the elements and said everyone is welcome at the table. I wondered to myself, am I welcome even though I no longer believe the way I was taught since childhood. For the first time in almost 20 years I went forward to take communion. We sang ""Take oh take me as I am."

Gary encouraged me to meet with Bev. Not too long after, I started to meet with Bev for spiritual direction. She gave me books to read on spiritual practice written by people such as Thomas Merton, Father Keating. I eventually joined a group of women who met for contemplative prayer on Wednesday mornings. During this time my mother's illness became acute. I spent the first nine months of 2000 traveling back and forth from Portland to care for her. She died in September of 2000.

I was still leery of Christianity and wondered how intelligent people could believe the stories in the bible. Then Bev told me about a book by Marcus Borg, reading the Bible Again for the First Time, and intrigued by the picture on the cover. When I started to read the book, it was as though he was talking directly to me. Dick's sermons, the women's retreats, and meeting with Bev all had an influence on me. I was done with dogmas and masculine references, there is an alternative which involves inclusiveness, the goodness of people, and a deep abiding love for all creation.

LIVING IN A SHRINE, COMPLETING THE CIRCLE

After my daughter's graduation from high school Gary and I decide it is time to move back to Portland and eventually move into my childhood home. The following is a conversation my daughter and I had in the kitchen:

"I noticed you replaced the white security door with one in brown. You're getting ready to paint Grandma Beth's house a color aren't you Mom?" asks Rebecca from her perch on the counter in her favorite corner of the kitchen. My 21-year-old daughter, home for Christmas break, is relaxed in baggy navy blue pants and T-shirt covered with a grey zip up sweatshirt, the hood pulled over auburn corkscrew curls.

"Haven't decided." I move back and forth in a narrow triangle between the refrigerator where I pull out a carton of eggs, the milk warming on the cook top, and a large metal container of flour near the sink, "The security door is brown because the color is more compatible with the new back door. I tried to match the old doors and trim in the house."

As if on cue, my husband Gary, a plastic bag of crickets for Enrique in his hand,

pushes open the redwood stained back door. In search of new color ideas, I try to engage him, "Gary, when we paint the house, what do you think of Texas Leather? I like the way it set off the land-scape around our house on Bainbridge."

Gary, always the diplomat, ignores my question, "MaryLouise, are you and Rebecca making your Mother's delicious cinnamon rolls?

"Yes. Do I see vultures circling?"

Gary's whole face lights up. "I need to go up to my office to check a few things. Don't forget to let me know when the rolls are ready."

My next strategy, focus on the task at hand, "Is Grandma's recipe on the counter behind you Rebecca?"

"You can't paint the house a color, it has always been white. I'm sure Aaron and even Gary would agree." Responds Rebecca's in an indignant tone while she hands over Mother's handwritten roll recipe.

Which Gary? I say.

Gary 2 of course. Your Gary goes along with you even when he disagrees.

I bemoan the confusion of two Gary's in our family, father and son, while I count ten cups of flour then fire back, "I didn't know any of you cared. You're away at college, Aaron lives in Pittsburgh, and Gary is in New Orleans."

"We care. It's bad enough that Grandpa Roland ripped out the kitchen."

We give each other sorrowful looks then direct our gaze to shaker style cherry cabinets, recessed can lights, a modern greenhouse window, and clunky microwave mounted too low over the cook top. Our minds drift to familiar images of pale yellow painted doors and drawers with sleek chrome handles, a window flanked with curved display shelves, jelly jar light fixtures, and homemade curtains decorated with embroidered daisies to match the yellow, green, and white daisy wallpaper.

"I miss the kitchen too." I say with a sigh, "It was the heart of the house. That's why Grandpa changed it when he married Marie after Mother died. At least the cupboard doors are still stacked above the garage and the grey Formica table occupies the same spot over there by the back door."

"Is it possible to recreate Grandma's kitchen?"

"I'd like to, but not without a lot of money and effort. Don't worry yet about the house color Sweet Pea, we won't need to paint for a few years. Now let's catch up with your last four months at art school in Santa Fe and bake Grandma's cinnamon rolls."

I hear Mother say, "You can please some of the people some of the time, but you can't please all the people all the time."

Remodel a revered shrine – a tricky proposition. Not everyone embraces change. Even my sister Judy who claims no emotional attachment said, "You always wanted to live in the house and then you changed everything. It doesn't matter to me, but it doesn't make sense."

No one complained about the deletion of Marie's decorating touches. Dad's second wife covered the walls with flowers in Easter egg colors. The children approved when we removed wall-to-wall carpet from honey colored oak floors. Our collaboration with Alice on interior colors, River Gorge Gray, Wethersfield Moss, Carolina Gull, Harvest Time, and Audubon Russet, was well received. I like to think we released hidden potential.

Cleared, cleaned, painted, and polished the house glows. Layers removed, positive energy restored. A fresh start for the house. A fresh start for MaryLouise and Gary.

Postscript: Mary Louise and I refurbished the home and made it our own. Mary Louise found her grandmother's postcard collection and Judy allowed her to have copies of Beth and Joe's letters. The house, the family research, a trip with her daughter to Montana, combined with a feeling of wholeness inspired Mary Louise to write this story. She came around full circle and was studying to be a Spiritual Director at the time of her sudden and unexpected death. Her soul and spirit are alive and well for those of us who love her.

Mary Louise is the most loving, gifted, spiritual, creative, passionate, beautiful and smartest person I will ever know. Our love for each other was beyond measure. It seems only fitting to conclude with three of her very special writings. The first is a love poem she wrote for me. The second is her Centering Poem and finally is her "Rule of Life". I will conclude by saying I love you sweetie with all of my heart your friend and lover forever. Gary

Dear Friend,
Walk with me
Where sea washes sand;
We shall bathe in solitude,
Together.

Confidante,
Listen with me
While sea whispers stories;
We shall share secrets,
Together.

Fun-Lover,
Laugh with me
When sea skips stones;
We hall touch happiness,
Together.

Companion,
Sit with me
While sea shimmers sunlight;
We shall forget time,
Together.

Faithful Partner,
Stay with me
Watch sea swallow fire,
We shall embrace life
Together.

Beloved,
Love with me
Where sea washes sand,
We shall be an ocean,
Together.

Yours Always, ML

Centering

There is chaos on the table,
it is my life.
Books, photographs, memories,
carefully selected, thoughtfully arranged.
The
past
piled
up.
The future waiting to be found.

In the clutter on the table,
is my heart.
How long has it been there, why couldn't I see it?
Looking without seeing.
Listening without hearing.
Knowing without understanding.

In the confusion on the table,
is my hope.
Only I can tell the story, only I can find the meaning.
I look and see visions.
I listen and hear poetry.
I know and understand love.

There is a feast on the table,
it is my life.
Books, photographs, memories,
carefully selected, thoughtfully arranged.
The
past
opened
up.
The future found.

My eager heart emerges
like a butterfly
trapped too long
in the threads of a wasted cocoon.
I leave behind
what I have been for everyone else
to become
what I am for myself.

Mary Louise Ott June 2000

MARY LOUISE'S RULE OF LIFE

With humility I co-create space to hold:

Mutual Trust

Generous Acceptance

Inner Mystery

Holy Imperfection

Unfolding Journey

Beauty in All Creation

A Sense of Wonder

Wholehearted Life, Love, and Laughter

Divine Presence

Peace

MaryLouise Ott
October 2015

Mary Louise and family home are under construction 1950. Beth Ott in the photo is pregnant.

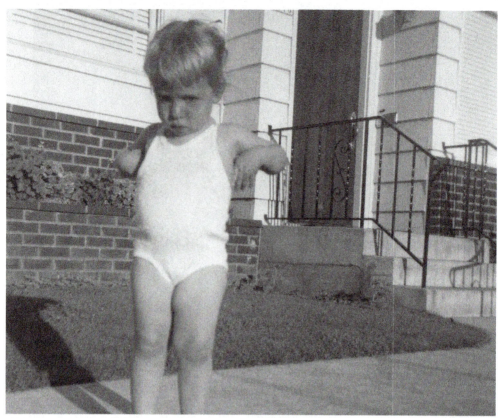

Compare the two photos and you can see the child in the adult Mary Louise

Childhood photos of Mary Louise

Childhood photos of Mary Louise

Piano lessons with Hal Howarth (Gary's Dad)

Mary Louise, Judy, & Beth having breakfast

Mary Louise picking berries

Beth & Roland Ott, Mary Louise, & Judy

Mary Louise drying dishes

Mary Louise and her Mother at Easter

Family Home 1950's

Mary Louise and Barbie's Wedding

Mary Louise and her Mother at Easter

Mary Louise's Grandparents Fenton & Mae Belle Roscoe

Joe McAllister & Beth Roscoe's Wedding

Christmas- Roland & Beth Ott, Gary Howarth, Judy Orem, Mike Small, Frank & Peter Orem, Mary Louise

Washington Park - see the Dangerous Pursuit Chapter

Left to Right: Nina & Hal Howarth, Gary II, Gary Howarth, Mary Louise Ott, Rebecca Katz, Arron Katz, Beth & Roland Ott (Mary Louise and Gary's Wedding Photo)

Mary Louise & Gary's Wedding Anniversary at the Bay House

Blythe Dolores Utz wearing the wedding dress Mary Louise created for her

Dottie Mae- Mary Louise's alter ego gave humorous presentations at the Kitsap Regional Library. Dottie Mae was a hoot and quite a character.

Left to Right: Gary Howarth, Mary Louise Ott, Elizabeth McKee Katz, Arron Katz, Rebecca Katz, Elise Dietrich, Gary Howarth II (Aaron & Elizabeth's Wedding)

Mary Louise's Art - Colored Pencil on Black Paper

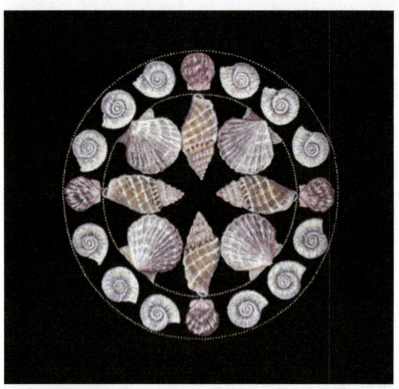

Mary Louise's Art - Colored Pencil on Black Paper

Mary Louise's Art - Colored Pencil on Black Paper

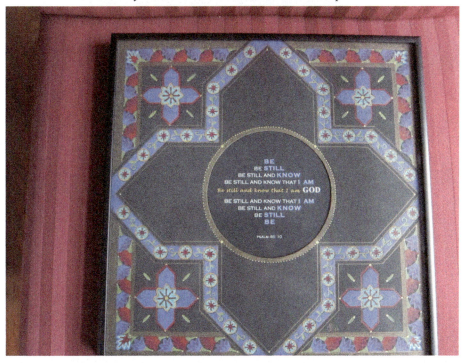

Mary Louise's Spiritual Art

A Peace Mobile created by Mary Louise

Mary Louise created a Sacred Space for a Franciscan Spiritual Retreat

Mary Louise hand stitched two quilts as a wedding present for each son.

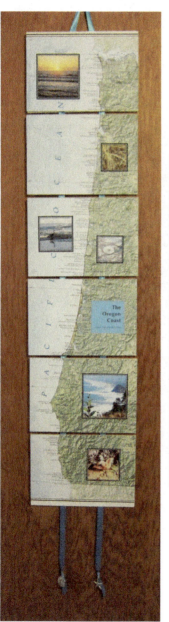

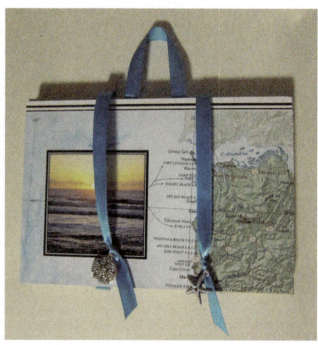

Mary Louise created these postcards for a charity auction in Scotland. Each postcard has a portion of a love poem written to her husband. The entire poem is included in this book.

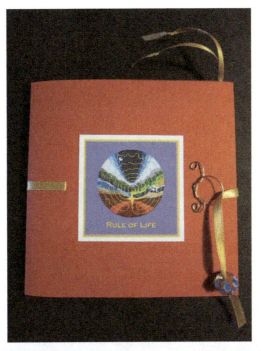

Mary Louise created a Rule of Life carousel book for each participant in the Spiritual Director's Training Program

Shrine at the Little Reservoir a sacred place Mary Louise enjoyed visiting

Mt Tabor's Little Reservoir a place where Mary Louise would meditate and reflect

Mary Louise & Rebecca on an Eastern Oregon trip

Rebecca's Graduation from College with her Father (Richard Katz)

Mary Louise & Gary at Tent Rocks New Mexico

Mary Louise's Garden

Mary Louise & Her Pumpkins

Mary Louise on the bridge near "Frog Land" at Neskowin

Mary Louise & Gary sitting on the balcony of Room 18 at Pacific Sands, Neskowin

Mary Louise, Vivian (Gary II's daughter) & Aaron Katz- Christmas 2014

Mary Louise sitting on a rock at Neskowin September, 2015

Mary Louise and Gary by the Big Rock at the north end of Neskowin Beach September, 2015

CPSIA information can be obtained
at www.ICGtesting.com
Printed in the USA
LVOW02*0218060817
543454LV00001BA/1/P